The Reverse Um

Stanislav Rudnitskiy

The Reverse Umbrella Company Concept

A qualitative study approaching export promotion on the basis of a novel concept targeting Vietnamese SMEs

Social Sciences Series

Impressum / Imprint

Bibliografische Information der Deutschen Nationalbibliothek: Die Deutsche Nationalbibliothek verzeichnet diese Publikation in der Deutschen Nationalbibliografie; detaillierte bibliografische Daten sind im Internet über http://dnb.d-nb.de abrufbar.

Bibliographic information published by the Deutsche Nationalbibliothek: The Deutsche Nationalbibliothek lists this publication in the Deutsche Nationalbibliografie; detailed bibliographic data are available in the Internet at http://dnb.d-nb.de.

Coverbild / Cover image: www.ingimage.com

Verlag / Publisher:
AV Akademikerverlag GmbH & Co. KG
Heinrich-Böcking-Str. 6-8, 66121 Saarbrücken, Deutschland / Germany
Email: info@akademikerverlag.de

Herstellung: siehe letzte Seite /
Printed at: see last page
ISBN: 978-3-639-47051-2

Abstract

This qualitative study approaches export promotion on the basis of a novel concept targeting small and medium sized enterprises on a corporate level.

As proven by various studies and reinforced throughout this research, small and medium sized enterprises worldwide are experiencing severe difficulties with the initial step to overseas markets. Especially, in developing countries framework conditions and internal barriers pose great hurdles to internationalization.

For this reason, the following pages represent an attempt to apply the Umbrella Company Concept to the internationalization of Vietnamese small and medium sized enterprises by reversing its principle. Thereby, a step by step approach to the concept provides the reader with a theoretical and practical perspective.

Through interviewing valuable experts in this field, significant differences between potential trade partners are confirmed and reveal several severe barriers to the establishment of international operations.

Going further, insights on how to overcome obstacles and barriers are gained and developed in theory as well as in practice. Among others, the study reinforces the notion of interrelation between risk, control and resource commitment from the perspective of small and medium sized enterprises. The accompanying case of Vietnamese Trung Kien Group serves as an ongoing vivid practical example.

This research is a profound proof to an existing issue and manages to reinforce as well as reveal important insights pushing the development and practical application of the Reverse Umbrella Company Concept.

Abbreviations

EPP   Export Promotion Programme

MNE   Multinational Enterprise

EPO   Export Promotion Programs

SME   Small and Medium Enterprises

RUCC   Reverse Umbrella Company Concept

USP   Unique Selling Proposition

OSEC   Office Suisse d'Expansion Commerciale

SIPPO   Swiss Import Promotion Programme

SPOC   Single Point of Contact

Table of contents

Table of Figures

Table of Appendices

1. Introduction

1.1. Route Map

The **introduction** provides the reader with a content related overview and framework of this research enabling to understand the **context** of the study. Further, this section leads the reader towards the comprehension of the underlying problem and how the **research question** attempts to solve it.

The **methodology section** explains the research from a scientific perspective highlighting the overall research strategy and providing details about **data collection, analysis** and the research **limitations**.

Subsequently, a brief overview about **existing knowledge** in the field of **internationalization** is provided, whereas only literature that is relevant to this study in terms of contextual understanding and its relation to the overall research goal is examined. Resulting from the gained insights **a contextual framework** with the purpose to provide guidance during data analysis and interpretation is introduced.

Thereafter, a **market analysis** is conducted to provide the reader with an exemplary approach towards the application of the RUCC. This section serves as an enhancer for the practical understanding of the RUCC and provides the basis for the interpretation of the research findings in the discussion and analysis section.

The **Findings section** clusters all gained data in subtopics and provides the reader with a detailed description of all data obtained through this research.

In the next step, **all data is evaluated** and brought into a logical order while applying it to the RUCC and providing ideas for **further scientific approaches** and practical implications.

Finally, the research is **reviewed** providing an overview of major findings and critically reflecting the overall **success** and value of this study.

1.2. Context

This Master Thesis is contextually related to a KTI[1] project serving the goal to research an innovative market entry and export method through the establishment of umbrella companies in the target countries. "The project includes the conceptualization and testing of a new innovative concept for low-cost market entry and rapid internationalization of at least 20 Swiss SMEs and start-up companies in the OSEC selected priority countries Indonesia, Kazakhstan, Thailand and Vietnam. The Institute of Management [of the FHNW] conducts applied research to the conceptual foundation and adaptation to local conditions. OSEC supports the selection of the SMEs and the execution of the empirical studies. The concept is based on the founding of Umbrella Companies invented by United Machinery with partners in target countries. This innovation decreases market entry costs by 40-70% compared to conventional concepts. It also speeds up the realization of export by 6-12 months with reduced risks. In the last phase of the project, the transferability of the results is tested for other countries and conclusions for strategies and instruments of export promotion will be developed." (FHNW, 2012). The overall goal is finding

---

[1] Swiss Commission for Technology and Innovation (http://www.kti.admin.ch/)

novel internationalization concept that addresses the special needs of SMEs and provides assistance.

1.3. Definitions

Internationalization

Since a single, universally accepted, definition of the term "internationalization" remains exclusive and authors differ in focus, for this research the "perhaps most useful" (Coviello and McAuley, 1999:224-225) definition of Bearnish (1990:77) will be used:

He defines internationalization as "...the process by which firms both increase their awareness of the direct and indirect influence of international transactions on their future, and establish and conduct transactions with other countries."

SME

For the definition of SMEs the Recommendation 2003/361/EC by the European Commission has been chosen: "The category of micro, small and medium-sized enterprises (SMEs) is made up of enterprises which employ fewer than 250 persons and which have an annual turnover not exceeding 50 million euro, and/or an annual balance sheet not exceeding 43 million euro." (Extract of Article 2 of the Annex of Recommendation 2003/361/EC) (EC, 2005) However, considering the labor intensive and far less technologized working situation in Asian countries, and in particular in Vietnam, the author adjusts the maximal number of employees to 300 people. (Ministry of Planning and Investment Vietnam, 2001)

1.4. Problem Statement

The Goal of this Master Thesis Research Project is to reverse the described principle finding a way to modify the Umbrella Company Concept promoting the internationalization of Vietnamese companies to Switzerland and explain this approach on the basis of Trung Kien, a Vietnamese SME producing special purpose bags for various industries.

This research is conducted in a timely manner as export promotion programs in developed countries become very common supporting the growth and internationalization of SMEs and large multinational enterprises (MNE). Those programs are largely financed by government agencies and business foundations which can put enterprises from developing countries into a disadvantageous position when promoting their products worldwide. (Spence, 2003; Genctürk and Masaaki, 2001) Especially, SMEs in developing economies struggle with problems connected to knowledge, technology and capital accumulation which create significant barriers to exploring foreign markets (Jaklic, 1998).

On the other hand, the need of finding new products and trustworthy suppliers for the domestic market can be a challenge for local (e.g. Swiss) enterprises. To tackle this issue several European governments have introduced import promotion programs / agencies that connect importers with sustainable suppliers and keep them abreast of current trends and innovations with a high market potential in Europe. An example of such an organization is the Swiss Import Promotion Programme (SIPPO).[2] (SIPPO, 2012) However, this is a one-sided approach where the promoting agency carries out the decisive power. An SME striving to internationalize can

---

[2]Website: http://importers.sippo.ch/en

easily be overseen and can barely influence the decision of the respective agency / promotion programme. (Francis and Dodd, 2004; Alvarez, 2004; Wilkinson, 2000) Therefore, it is important to find ways how SMEs can promote themselves despite the lack of resources.

In this context, researchers have found out that, supported by new communication and transportation technologies, globalization of markets and increased cultural awareness throughout the world (Aution, 2005; Oviatt and McDougall, 2005), SMEs do not follow traditional internationalization theories, such as the Uppsala model (Johanson and Vahlne 1977, Johanson and Wiedersheum-Paul, 1975). Hence, it is to be researched what paths SMEs with the ability and goal to internationalize can take. Thereby, an existing and working concept of alternative internationalization, the UCC, is used as basis. The idea of the UCC is kept, whereas the direction of internationalization is changed.

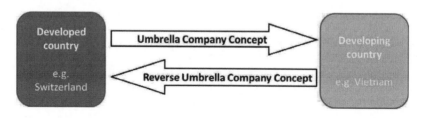

Figure 1 Comparison of UCC and RUCC

All in all, the presented arguments lead to the conclusion that research on individual SME internationalization with the goal of finding a new internationalization approach has to be conducted. Therefore, this study attempts to explore a new form of internationalization and explain it using the case of the Vietnamese Trung Kien Group.

1.5. Research Questions

How does the Umbrella Company Concept has to be modified in order to provide support for Vietnamese SMEs internationalizing to Switzerland?

A. What is the basis for internationalizing to Switzerland?
B. What factors have to be modified for a successful adaption of the concept?
C. How can Vietnamese SMEs be supported during the internationalization?

2. Research Design

2.1. Type of Design

This research pursues a qualitative approach aiming at gathering rich, deep data in an explorative way. Hence, the goal of researching a novel concept, such as the Reverse Umbrella Company Concept can be pursued ideally with the freedom of flexibly adjusting the concrete research direction based on the gathered data in real time. This implies the adjustment of research sub-questions based on the gathered data, however not changing the overall research goal. Generally, the complexity of conceptualizing and implementing such a concept in a highly saturated market requires a method that can break down complex structures and link them to practice, facilitating theory development and further research in this area (Bryman and Bell, 2011).

Moreover, the research pursues a simultaneously deductive and inductive approach: on the one hand, based on the literature review the research tests the applicability of existing internationalization theories, such as the

Network Approach and aim to approve or revoke insights provided through other studies applying them towards the RUCC. On the other hand, the attempt to develop a theoretical framework fitting the gathered data and leading to broader generalizations is made. Thereby, tracking back and forth between theory and data enables the creation of connections developing or enriching existing knowledge with new insights (Bryman and Bell, 2011).

As an accompanying case Vietnamese Trung Kien will be used to support the research with a practical example and provide practical approaches to occurring ideas, inputs, issues, etc. As a result, rich data for the applicability of the concept, possible ways of adjustment and further research projects will be collected.

The literature review serves as a basis for the analysis of the data and its relation to the overall research topic. In essence, the five fields of the literature review are chosen to accommodate the major aspects of an Asian SME-internationalization to a developed country economy. For instance, the section "SME Internationalization" incorporates research on how this process is different for SMEs as compared to multinational enterprises. Moreover, every literature review section attempts to focus on research that is relevant to the thesis research goal and the particular case of a Vietnamese company internationalizing to a mature European market, such as Switzerland. Thereby, the five sections are designed to complement one another building upon each other. For instance, Internationalization draws the big picture the research is conducted in. Subsequently, it is related to SMEs and further on internationalization modes drawing attention on export afterwards. This establishes a stringent literature analysis which in turn provides a structural basis for the final data analysis. The conceptual framework unites and concentrates this basic thought.

2.2. Data Collection

The primary source of data collection will be interviews. Thereby, 3 expert interviews are being conducted to obtain insightful experimental knowledge, anecdotal evidence and find new directions of research. All of the experts have experience in working with internationalization and its promotion. The expert round can contribute to the topic from various important perspectives enhancing the quality of the gathered data. Certainly, only experts with a positive attitude towards the promotion of internationalization and import/export through novel concepts have been chosen for this research. This is to constrain the data variance on the one hand and to maintain the progressive spirit of this research on the other hand.

Prof. Dr. X (name anonymized) has worked has expertise of the Swiss and German markets and consulted Asian companies with the wish to enter the European market for over a decade. Dr. Nguyen The Vinh has worked in the internationalization field for over 2 years, has worked with the Umbrella Company Concept and is member of several Vietnamese SME associations and promotion/consulting functions (CV on CD). The third interviewee required to remain anonymous and is therefore not mentioned by name or function in any part of the report. However, the third interviewee has significant experience and a professional status with a high importance for this research.

Generally, the chosen experts contribute to the research from the perspective of an Asian country, the perspective of a corporate level and a governmental perspective in a Western target country for the RUCC.

Two interviews are semi-structured allowing the interviewer and interviewee to flexibly express their thoughts. Despite the semi-structured approach interview guides have been designed to make the gathered data qualitatively reliable and comparable. An interview guide is created providing the interviewer with an outline of topics to be discussed and a broad interview road map. The first interview with Prof. Dr. X (name anonymized) serves as a pilot to determine possible weaknesses, such as doubling of questions, loss of the central theme or inexplicit questions, but also to integrate new ideas and lines of questioning. Concretely, the pilot interview revealed the necessity to detail question 3 in the core question section and develop a new question 4 (*"How do SMEs internationalize nowadays?)* with 4 sub-questions to make a clearer distinction in opinion today and in a future outlooks and determine motives that would be transferable onto the RUCC. Further, a question about barriers for internationalization has been added to create an awareness of problems and lead the interviewee towards developing an opinion about the RUCC and potential weaknesses as well as advantages. Generally, the pilot interview revealed that interviewees were drifting away from the actual goal of the research. Hence, a more detailed and explicit method of questioning has been chosen for the second version of the interview guide. Further details of adjustment can be observed through direct comparison of the interview guides in the appendix and on the CD.

The interviewees have a great deal of leeway in how to reply. Questions may not follow exactly the way outlined in the schedule. Questions that are not included in the guide may be asked as the interviewer picks up on things said by interviewees (Bryman and Bell, 2011:467). The expert interviews are of up to two hours duration and conducted via Skype, telephone and email. The interview with Dr. Nguyen The Vinh is conducted via Email due to geographical distance, time zone difference and private difficulties of the interviewee. The rest of the data is collected though secondary data such as provided company documents, online research and literature review.

For reasons of privacy requirement through the interviewees, interviews are not recorded. This measure purposefully deviates from the overall research requirements assuring the needed openness and detail of the answers and a truly expert opinion. Hence, the low number of interviews can assured to be qualitatively rich enough for the execution of the proposed research strategy.

2.3. Data Analysis

As preparation for the data analysis the interviews will be summed up as detailed as possible (notes in the appendix). Subsequently, the contextual content will be characterized and grouped according to major areas of interest respective research questions and hypothesis. Thereby, alike coding with the help of software (e.g. Atlas.ti) the same information can be considered as relevant for generally every category and group. The advantage of avoiding the use of coding software is the possibility to assure that contextual statements are not being interchanged or incorrectly interpreted in the analysis section. This allows making connections to the literature review and market analysis and helps avoiding one typical limitation of grounded theory as described by Bryman and Bell, 2011: "The time taken to transcribe tape recordings of interviews [...] can make it difficult for researchers [...] to carry out a genuine grounded theory analysis with its constant interplay of data collection and conceptualization." (page 591). Hence, the risk that contextual connections and therefore important information is lost in the coding scheme is minimized. (Coffey and Atkinson, 1996)

Additionally, secondary data, gained through access to company and project documents and the literature review, will be analyzed to confirm, reject or neutralize gained insights as well as support the creation of interview guides.

The findings are clustered in logical subtopics to structure the data, but are not explicitly related to a particular interviewee to assure that anonymity is maintained at all times and data cannot be attributed to the participants. In addition, eight hypotheses are derived from the literature review and answered with the help of the findings leading over to answering the overall research question.

2.4. Ethical Issues

Generally, every research being conducted faces certain ethical issues that ought to be considered, evaluated and weighted. Basic ethical guidelines such as the United States Belmont Report (1988), Australia's National Statement of Research Involving Humans (NHMRC, 1999) or Great Britain's Research Ethics Framework (ESRC) have been established in different countries to provide participants with a set of rights and the researcher with responsibilities. Most of the existing frameworks point out justice, beneficence and respect as the guiding ideas for ethical consideration. (Lindorff, 2007)

Justice, according to Aristotle, is "that which is lawful and that which is equal and fair" (1982, p.257). Relating this principle to business research it can mean that certain groups involved in the research should not take the burden of participation and disclosure, whereas others profit from it, i.e. the effort and use from the research ought to be equally distributed. Although this research is guided by complete justice and attempts to assure the equal treatment of all participants, certain discrepancies, depending on the perspective, are possible. On the one hand, Vietnamese Trung Kien bears the burden of serving as a role model and case for this research disclosing internal company data, risking to have invested time and money without all of it paying off at the end. Other SMEs will profit from mistakes being made and adjustments being implemented over time. On the other hand, Trung Kien might perceive the amount of work being invested in its internationalization and the involvement of several parties as a reason to feel pressured to actually internationalize without being in any way ready for that step.

However, this research is guided by the idea of creating mutual benefits by providing a new model of export promotion which traditionally opens new markets for the exporter, securing its prosperity and growth and provides the supply chain of the target country with new, sometimes better, suppliers. Moreover, through the possibility of anonymization research participants, i.e. the interviewed experts are given the possibility of minimizing harm or discomfort of their own and the organizations they work for. Further, the right of privacy and preservation of face is especially important for research conducted in Asian countries. The risk of "loosing face" is given in the Vietnamese culture and ought to be avoided. Nevertheless, it is present and the involvement of case of Trung Kien could harm the reputation of this family owned business as well as its business relations / partners. Therefore, confidentiality and anonymity is a highly respected right of every participant of this research and flexibly adjusted upon request. Most of the expert participants in this research have chosen to stay anonymous and wished not to reveal sensitive key data and numbers about their work and companies. However, concrete numbers and key figures have been mentioned in throughout all interviews it was agreed not to reveal it in written form in order to prevent an identification of the participants through surrounding insiders.

The confidentiality of collected data is also important when considering that this research is conducted in the framework of a master thesis and is therefore submitted to the master committee for evaluation. Therefore, participants are informed that two people will be reading and evaluating this report and that its defense is open for public. Participants have further been informed that the report might be published and hence accessible to the public. All of these measures have been taken prior to the research so that choices about anonymization and confidentiality could be made prior to participation and data disclosure.

2.5. Limitations

This section is divided into 3 parts answering different perspectives of limitations: methodology, data, and analysis.

Methodology

Generally, several arguments of choosing quantitative research over qualitative are possible at this point. However, this section attempts to point out the most severe limitations. The case of Trung Kien which accompanies the research as an ongoing example could be extended to a case study research approach and where the company is accompanied during the process of internationalization from the first step to the last. This would provide a practical test of the RUCC and by far more insights to the practical adaptation of the Umbrella Company Concept. Further, the short time frame given by this master thesis module is constraining the amount of information collected and analyzed. Moreover, the decision to use to use expert interviews as the primary source of data collection bears certain limitations: firstly, interviewees are not chosen by an objective criterion, but rather upon the researcher's knowledge about their experience and their availability. Secondly, the contextual nature of opinions can impact the applicability of the outcome to a variety of cases and thereby the true insight. This and the limited number of experts have an impact on the generalizability and validity of the results. Third, the semi-structured nature of the interviews leaves a certain amount of openness towards adaptation of the research questions and concept. However, this can also lead to a loss of focus. Interviews can come out quite differently and lead to inconsistent results. The anonymity of certain interviewees and the choice to avoid transcribing lower the possibility to reproduce this research, hence the comparability of the outcome.

Data

Part of the arguments discussed above, are also valid for the limitations of the collected data. The information collected through the literature review is fairly limited due to the given time frame and chosen focus. Further, the interviews could have been extended to longer periods of sequential interviews in order to gather more in depth information from each interviewee. Certainly, the same can be argued about the amount of interviews. Moreover, the basic positive attitude of the interviewees towards the RUCC could lead to bias in their answers and reduce the quality of data through factors such as enthusiasm. As one expert has chosen to stay anonymous and not reveal any key data, the quality of the data is impeded. Moreover, the email interview with Dr. Vinh is certainly not detailed enough to add the wished amount and quality of data to the research. Doubtlessly, the collection of data is biased since connections to existing knowledge of the interviewer are automatically made and many questions are asked in in the heat of the moment.

Analysis

The analysis of this research is limited by the overall time constrains and disadvantages associated with the methodology. The desired induction of theory is quite challenging, because of the danger of losing track when going back and forth between data and theory to establish new principles. The potential to connect all and everything is nearly unlimited. Further, the mentioned context could be a disadvantage at the same time: contextual relations could be interpreted incorrectly or information could have been lost in the notes or overheard during the interview without the possibility to double check in the recordings. Generally, correlation of information does not explain its causation and therefore could be integrated incorrectly.

3. Literature Review

For conducting a comprehensive literature review the following concepts have been identified as important to the research topic, a Reverse Umbrella Company Concept (RUCC):

- Internationalization
- SME internationalization
- Export promotion
- Market entry
- Vietnam in terms of economically relevant indicators

Generally, all sources of literature and research (printed and online) are considered. However, the high amount of online sources can be interpreted as a result of the timeliness and current market trend regarding this particular field.

Conceptually, the literature review will pursue the goal of providing a brief overview over each concept subsequently relating it to the research issue, thereby leading the reader to the development of this issue and the research gap.

3.1. Internationalization

The Internationalization of companies is a phenomenon that has been extensively researched. Early thinkers, such as Adam Smith, Heckser-Ohlin and David Ricardo have introduced their thoughts about internationalizing businesses to the outside world. (Fillis 2001) Due to soon occurring limitations of international trade theories two economic schools of thought, the neoclassical and classical, have evolved. Producing concepts, such as the Product-life-cycle-theory, the Internationalization Theory, The Industrial Organization Theory and the Eclectic Paradigm all of them were lacking "dynamic considerations". (Welch and Luostarinen, 1988) Consequently, a more dynamic, behavioral approach to internationalization was found in the early 1970s. The stage theories allowed drawing more attention on internationalization processes of SMEs. Today, the Uppsala Model, innovation related approaches and the Network Approach are considered as the modern theories towards internationalization. However, the Uppsala Model is the most popular and widely researched internationalization approach. On the basis, is the thought that firms pass through an incremental process of increasing international commitment (Johanson and Vahlne 1977). However, empirical evidence of several studies does not support this model: Andersen (1993), for instance, criticizes the lack of explanation. Other critics argue against the step-by-step character and the denegation of interdependencies between markets and actors. (Chetty and Capmbell, 2003; Hollensen, 2001; Crick 1995)

The Innovation-related Internationalization Models appeared in the late 1970s and analyzed the development of export activities mainly focusing on SMEs (Andersen, 1993). According to a comprehensive review of the most important innovation related models by Leonidou and Katsikeas (1996) this approach can be characterized by a number of fixed, export-related sequential stages (Ruzzier et al., 2006). Thereby, most models differ solely in terminology and number of stages. Miesenbock (1998) and Andersen (1993) criticize the vague theoretical basis and difficulty to distinguish between stages stating that too little attention is paid to the duration and operational activities.

The Network Approach applied a network perspective on the basis of the Uppsala Model by relating it with gradual learning and the development of market knowledge through interaction within business networks. (Johanson and Mattson, 1993; McAuley, 1999) A firm gains access to assets by building relationships with other firms such as suppliers, customers and competitors (Rutihinda, 2008). Today, much of the network-based research draws attention on the management of international relationships. What seems to be neglected is the strategic position and influence of individuals, especially in the SME's internationalization process. (Ruzzier et al., 2006) For SME's in catching-up economies networks can be of particular relevance in overcoming problems of knowledge, technology and capital accumulation (Jaklic, 1998). Moreover, Network theory can provide insight in how resources, actors and activities within networks affect the different dimensions of a SME's internationalization (Hakansson and Snehota, 1995). Research in this area has proven that relationships are a basis for the internationalization process (Axelsson and Johanson, 1992; Jansson, 2007; Ford, 2002; Johanson and Vahle, 2003). However, network theory has been widely criticized for its lack of incorporating strategic aspects of internationalization (Rutihinda, 2008).

This criticism leads to another internationalization approach, the Resource-based Internationalization Theory. Within the field of strategic management it is largely based on the writings of Andrews (1995) & Chandler (1962) and Penrose's (1959) work. In its core, the firm's ability to attain and keep profitable market positions depends on its ability to gain and defend advantageous resource conditions (Conner, 1991). This highlights the importance of intangible knowledge-based resources in providing a competitive advantage (Ruzzier et. al., 2006). As a result, the understanding of a firm's diversification strategies internationalization being one of them has improved (Montgomery and Wernfelt, 1997).

The evolvement of network and resource-based perspectives appears to be going hand in hand. In both, internal and external resources are seen as constituting the total set of resources available the firm. (Ruzzier et. al., 2006) Moreover, both theories seem to be merging with the model proposed by Ahokangas (1998). The research of Ruzzier et. al. (2006), however, indicates the lack of research regarding SMEs from the resource-based perspective.

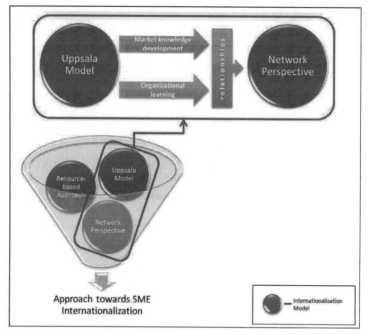

Figure 2 Classification of this research within Internationalization research

In this regard, Dunning (1993) stated that resource seeking, market seeking and efficiency seeking can be seen as the major motives for internationalization. However, theories have largely been used to explain internationalization processes of multinational enterprises. In fact, limited market power and resources attribute to major differences in internationalization of SMEs compared to MNCs which is while research on internationalization of SMEs has increased in recent years. (Seerat et. al., 2011) These insights lead to the following hypothesis: **Hypothesis 1: The support of SME internationalization through networks increases the success of internationalization attempts and confidence of Vietnamese SMEs.**

3.2. SME Internationalization

Moreover, SME internationalization is seen as eased by new communication and transportation technologies, globalization of markets and increased cultural awareness throughout the world (Aution, 2005; Oviatt and McDougall, 2005). As a result, several researchers came to the conclusion that SMEs do not follow traditional internationalization theories, such as the Uppsala model (Johanson and Vahlne 1977, Johanson and Wiedersheum-Paul, 1975). In 2004 a study by Leonidou classified internationalization barriers of SMEs as internal and external, whereas an OECD-APEC study on "Removing Barriers to SME Access to International Markets" in 2006 found out that internal barriers are perceived as greater hurdles. A study by the University of Otago supported this notion. As the top barriers limited financial recourse, limited access to capital, high costs of selling abroad, limited government assistance and limited knowledge of overseas market opportunities were identified (Shaw and Darroch, 2004).

Hypothesis 2: The need to overcome internal barriers prior to internationalization is highly important and rather underestimated.

Interestingly, numerous studies highlight the challenges faced by SMEs internationalizing, whereas very few provide meaningful comparisons of best practices across economies. (BDO Consultants, 2011) One of the most recent studies tackling this issue is the "Study on SME Internationalization Best Practices Across Selected APEC Economies" by Spring Singapore. Combined with the fact that SMEs do not follow traditional internationalization strategies an opportunity to research new models of internationalization arises (Johanson and Vahlne 1977).

In a study about SME internationalization and performance Beamish and Lu (2006) discovered that export activities facilitate growth, however negatively impact profitability. Researching a novel internationalization approach, the mentioned barriers and deviations from large companies ought to be considered and analyzed. This research ought to include how much internal and external barriers impact the internationalization of an SME.

Hypothesis 3: SMEs do not follow traditional models of internationalization and therefore are in need of novel supportive approaches.

3.3. Export Promotion

Generally, Export is seen as the easiest and fastest way of entering foreign markets due to the low levels of commitment and risk involved. (Beamish et. al., 2006) Since the Reverse Umbrella Company Concept is designed as a new form of export promotion this concept is of special interest to the literature review.

Importantly, most researchers outline the high importance of SMEs for modern, in particular Western, economies. For instance, approximately 90% of all companies in the EU can be characterized as small or medium according to the parameters of this research. (Demick et. al., 2000) Demick (2000) points out that many governments drive the economy towards export-led growth. Considering that a vast majority of SMEs worldwide perform modest on export, the importance and increased activity of export promotion organizations (EPOs) can be easily reasoned. Asian SMEs perform by far worse on export than their Western counterparts which increases the demand for promotional institutions or concepts. (Nazar and Saleem, 2009) As a result, many researches argue that EPO's work is important for SMEs as well as for a modern economy as a whole. (Demick et. al., 2000)

However, research has shown that SMEs and their export activities are confronted with several specific issues: for instance, the fact that SMEs still contribute less than 10% to national exports in advanced economies is conflicting with most government's focus of export and the high share of SME's contribution to economies (approx. 90%). (Demick et. al., 2000) Further, financial constraints, restricted access to experts and skilled personnel, limited scale of operations (Naidu and Prasad, 1994) and the absence of strategic thinking and planning (Mitchell and Bradley, 1986; Lyles et al., 1993) can be attributed to the issues SMEs are facing when engaging in export.

Hypothesis 4: Important internal barriers are the absence of strategic thinking and planning, limited scale of operations and restricted access to experts and skilled personnel.

Throughout the process of internationalization SMEs are in need of different types of export assistance (Johanson et. al., 1975; Cavusgil, 1980; Czinkota, 1982). Conventional EPOs that work with MNEs too, often apply measures that are not suitable for SMEs (Walters, 1983; Buckley, 1983). These facts impede the support through traditional EPO programs. Additionally, SME awareness of export support programs can be considered low (Bannock, 1987, Reid, 1984) as many EPOs are initially designed and advertised for large firms in advanced economies.

However, EPO programs also have been widely adopted and are being increasingly directed towards SMEs. Especially, Scandinavian countries seem to be on the top of these processes. Recently, Australian and New Zealand EPOs copied the Scandinavian model and developed it for their needs. (Cavusgil, 1990; Crick; 1995) These adaptations take different approaches, but commonly suggest developing in house export competencies trough consulting measures and group SMEs together for education and support purposes. (McNaughton and Bell, 1999) In the basis, this is similar to what the Reverse Umbrella Company Concept Suggests. Again, researchers point out that networks play an important role in the development of an export drive, but also and more importantly in the development of skills needed to succeed abroad (Dubini and Aldrich,

1991). As a result, the need for this network to be formalized is essential in researching concepts and developing export support approaches (Carson, 1993). Thereby, EPOs can play an important role through providing confidence, knowledge and export skills.

Hypothesis 5: Vietnamese SMEs need extensive consultative assistance in preparation for internationalizing to a Western market.

Gemunden (1991) and Wilkinson and Brouthers (2006) mention that research about SME export is to a wide extent empirical and descriptive lacking theory development attempts. Existing research looks at managerial attitudes, resources, the marketing mix et al. and remained empirical with increasing sophistication of methods and data sets. (Peng and Ilinitch, 1998; Gray, 1997; Dhanaraj and Beamish, 2003).

Wilkinson and Brouthers (2006) mention that accessing the possibilities and limitations of export promotions programs, it is important to consider barriers of export. They conclude that studies either look at structure and nature of barriers or on their influence during the export process of companies. However, "there seems to be no general agreement on the relative importance of the barriers in explaining export entry or expansion behavior of firms" (Ramaswami and Yang, 1990) Many studies outline the importance of managerial commitment to export and its decisive role pursuing an export strategy (Su'rez-Ortega, 2003, Bagchi-Sen, 1999). Moreover, many classifications of barriers have been developed over time: Seringhaus and Rosson (1989) define 4 categories (motivational, informational, operational, knowledge). Leonidou (2004) after having conducted a comprehensive analysis of 32 studies has identified 39 export barriers and categorized them in internal and external. In relation to Vietnam, many economic and political barriers, such as trade barriers, but also cultural barriers are being pointed out by researchers and will be mentioned in the Vietnam section of the Literature review.

In the past studies produced contradictory opinions on the effectiveness of export promotion programs (EPPs) (Wilkinson, T. and Brouthers, L., 2006). However, positive relationships between EPPs and a company's performance were found (Cavusgil and Jacob, 1987; Pointon, 1978). For instance, trade shows and trade missions have found to facilitate performance, because managers are able to acquire information about export markets and processes quickly. Other studies showed no connection of trade shows and managerial as well as company export performance (Seringhaus, 1986).

Many researchers highlight the positive effect of export on employment, foreign exchange revenues, prosperity and other economic factors increasing the competitiveness of market and firms. A 2001 study of 162 firms by Genctürk and Kotabe found that EPO services did not contribute to sales but enhanced competitive position of a firm. Moreover, committed exporters had easier access to cost benefits generated through EPPs. Lages and Montgomery (2001) found that companies receiving EPO services have a more profound pricing strategy and can adapt better to international markets. They found that international experience and industry competiveness strongly influence that success potential of EPPs.

All in all, several studies have proven that EPPs can be successful and effective under certain circumstances and conditions. However, the EPP's structure and commitment of the firm play key success of EPO services. (Wilkinson, T. and Brouthers, L., 2006) The issue of suitability of EPO services for the special needs of SMEs, the consequences of dealing with significant barriers and the role of networks will accompany the research and can ideally be described using the example of Trung Kien.

3.4. Market Entry

Existing literature covering market entry of firms is closely connected to research and publications about internationalization. Moreover, many times the reader will find that "market entry" and "internationalization" as terms are often interchangeable covering the same meaning or even purposefully used as synonyms. (Jansson and Sandberg, 2007) To make a clear distinction between the two terms in this paper, the internationalization section highlights the decision making process to internationalize, in other words the decision to move any amount of operational corporate activity (e.g. sales) beyond the border of the home country. Hence, market entry covers the process of making choices of how to internationalize and the difficulty of facing different barriers to internationalization.

Nowadays, most research conducted in this field concentrates on the question of how firms chose which entry mode to pursue during internationalization, given that they have a choice (Pan and Tse, 2000). Thereby, three schools of thought have taken hold: the first school considers overseas business operations to be inherently risky and threatening to the firm's stability. Therefore, this school suggests a gradual step by step involvement in foreign markets (Johanson and Vahlne, 1977, 1990). The idea is to start off with a very low resource commitment using as less financial, human and other resources as possible to minimize the risk of wasting them in an unsuccessful attempt to internationalize.

The second school of thought advocates the transaction cost perspective. In its basis stands the idea that firms naturally are going to keep those activities that create cost advantages towards other firms inside the company and perform them by themselves. In contrary, activities that can be performed better or cheaper by other firms are outsourced or subcontracted. The outsourced activities usually face one-time or/and reoccurring transaction costs for monitoring and controlling of the outsourced functions, network establishment, reorganization of the value chain and others. (Dunning, 1988; Pan and Tse, 2000)

The third school of thought focuses on location specific factors, basically arguing that non-production related costs (i.e. transaction costs) have increasing impact on entry mode choices (Pan and Tse, 2000).

Literature identifies several modes of entry depending on source and focus. The most common are exporting, licensing, franchising, contract manufacturing, joint ventures, wholly owned subsidiaries and strategic alliances (Agarwal and Ramaswami, 1992). According to the product life cycle hypothesis of Vernon (1966) a majority of the firms will chose exporting in the first place and continue the internationalization with market-seeking FDI, subsequently switching to cost-oriented FDI. Agarwal and Ramaswami (1992) argue that every choice of entry mode represents a compromise between the three attributes: amount of control, resource availability and risk. This kind of approach lies in the basis of the Reverse Umbrella Company Concept attempting to create a low risk and resource commitment entry mode through exporting. The compromise is the loss of certain control simultaneously minimizing the risk.

Regarding entry barriers several studies have been conducted. Karakaya and Stahl (1989) test six market entry barriers in consumer and industrial markets. These are cost advantages of incumbents, product differentiation of incumbents, capital requirements, consumer switching costs, access to distribution channels and government policy. The result of the study reveals that cost advantages of incumbents can be considered the most important barrier of all six. Among others, Porter (1980) and Shepherd (1979) stress that barriers put incumbents in an advantageous position over potential entrants to the market and thereby confirm the results of Karakaya and Stahl (1989). Therefore, this factor will play an important role in the market analysis section of this report. Many authors go further and identify cost advantages and above-average profitability of incumbents (Yip 1982a) (Mann, 1966) (Shepherd, 1979). Appendix 1 mentions a selection of barriers that have been identified by various researchers (Source: Karakaya und Stahl, 1989).

It is generally accepted that entry modes differ in amount of control firms have over their operations and the internationalization process in general (Anderson and Gatignon, 1986; Root, 1987). In this context, the research of Anderson and Gatignon (1986) concludes that the amount of control can increase a firm's commitment and level of involvement. Certainly, exceptions to this rule are known, however it has proved a valid generalization to make. Logically, firms will seek entry modes with a high level of involvement. But, when facing an "unacceptable" uncertainty level and risk, firms will try to reduce involvement and cut back resource commitment. In this case the might prefer to team up with outside agents, distributors or/and partners, thereby giving up control in order to reduce the risk of internationalization. (Erramilli and Rao, 1990) (Aharoni, 1966;

Mascarenhas, 1982) This is a key insight for this research since the Reverse Umbrella Company Concept is designed to reduce risk and resource commitment while making the trade-off of lessening control over the internationalization process.

Hypothesis 6: **The process of SME internationalization is accompanied by a trade-off between avoiding risk and maintaining high control over the own operations.**

Certain authors argue that choosing a difficult market first when internationalizing is more likely to reveal success potential, strengths, weaknesses and other factors of companies. This is best explained with the example of Chinese Haier. After changing the CEO Haier started manufacturing sophisticated product and soon came to the point of being ready for internationalization. When choosing which market to penetrate first Mr. Rumin, Haier CEO, decided for the United States - not for a geographically and culturally close market to China. He reasoned his decision as follows: "We believe that if we can succeed there, we can succeed in easier markets!". Basically, a company challenges itself to meet the highest quality and demand standards and develops know-how that would not develop by going into the Southeast Asian market. For the RUCC and Trung Kien this can serve as one of the motivators and sophistications entering the Swiss market. Moreover, this notion has already proven to work with Chinese Haier and any others and therefore can be seen as an anchor for the idea and the development of the RUCC.

3.5. Vietnam

This section provides a short overview over Vietnam's history and goes on with specific economic and cultural facts that are relevant to this research.

History

The Socialist Republic of Vietnam was founded in 1975 when Ho Chi Minh reunited the country under his communist leadership after the American forces had to withdraw from the country. Saigon was renamed to Ho Chi Minh City and regained its status as the country's commercial center. In 1986 the Vietnamese Communist Party officially launched Vietnams's "economic renovation" (Doi Moi) which led to the deregulation of prices, ended the collective agricultural system, introduced new FDI laws, launched policies towards the deregulation and convertibility of the Dong (local currency) and reduced subsidies to state enterprises. These measures helped Vietnam become the fastest-growing economy in the world at that time. From 1996 Vietnam's party continued with the transformation of the economy to a "market socialist" model under the control of the state.

Economy

Today, still 40% of the GDP is generated by state owned enterprises. However, the per capita GDP experienced a continuous growth since reforms in the 90s took effect (Fig. 3). Generally, Vietnam's economy is strongly export oriented with an increase by over 33% in 2011. This advancement was also due to Vietnam's membership in the WTO since 2007. With a median age of 28.2 years the population is very young which combined with the high life expectancy of 72.41 years creates a huge workforce (Fig. 3). The unemployment rate is at a low of 4.6% which ranks Vietnam 124th in

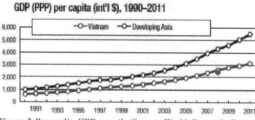

Figure 3 Per capita GDP growth (Source: World Economic Forum, 2012)

the world. Education is very good and one of the governments priorities, which explains rank 26 worldwide in primary education enrolment according to the Global Competitiveness Report 12/13.

However, the country faces challenges, such as one of the world's highest inflation rates averaging at 18% in 2011 and a huge trade deficit due to the export led

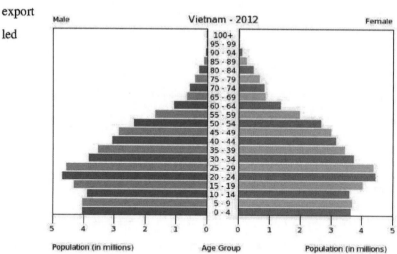

Figure 4 Vietnam's Demographics 2012 (Source: CIA World Factbook, 2012)

growth. According to the World Economic Forum and its Global Competitiveness Report 12/13 the major obstacle for business in Vietnam is the accessibly of financial resources and venture capital which is aggravated by the high inflation (Fig. 5).

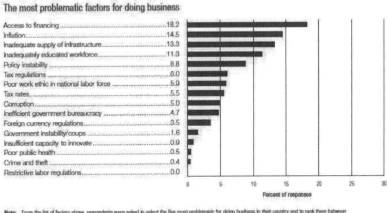

Figure 5 Most problematic factors for business (Source: Global Competitiveness Report 12/13)

SMEs account for roughly 97% of all businesses in the country and employ 77% of the workforce. According to the government more than 40% of the GDP is generated by SMEs. Figure 6 shows the rapid growth of newly registered SMEs in Vietnam. (CIA, 2012; Runckel, 2011; World Bank, 2012)

Among others the government, the Vietnam Chamber of Commerce and Industry, the Asian Development Bank and foreign governments, such as the German, have implemented a variety of support programs to improve the status of SMEs in Vietnam. However, there are severe issues such as the high interest rates for capital, a rapid increase in production costs and decline in profits according to a survey conducted by the VCCI on 360 businesses and 34 business associations nationwide. For instance, the survey revealed that 44% of businesses were borrowing from banks at interest rates of more than 18% a year. Some enterprises encountered interest rates of 20-27%.

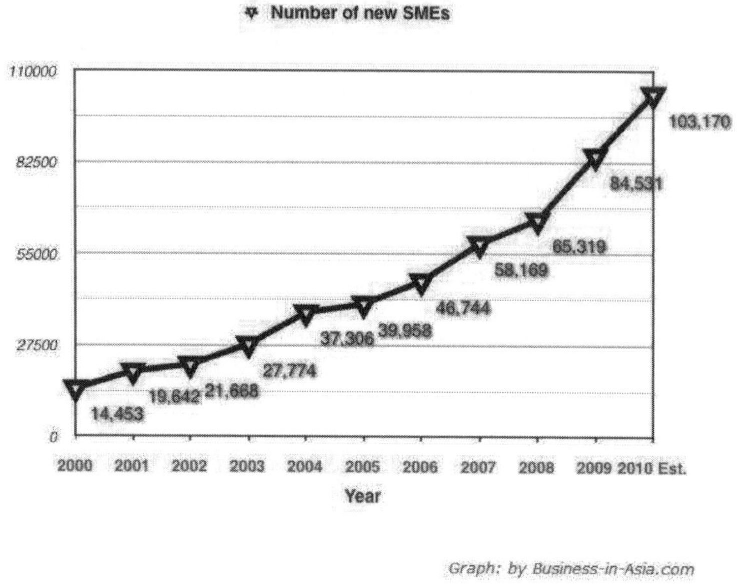

Figure 6 Number of SMEs from 2000 to 2010 (Source: Business in Asia, 2012)

State owned enterprises have significant advantages, such as longer terms and lower interest rates for credits without the need for mortgages. According to a survey by Thanh Hain Nguyen and others (2009) training and development programs for the development of managerial skills and know-how are present however fail to provide qualitatively high advisory and training. The study further revealed a lack of formal linkages among businesses that prevents the development of cooperation among potential production partners or SMEs that could cooperate along the value chain. According to the authors of the study this also causes uncertainty and risk perception when it comes to engaging in international business with foreign partners. Even though the government eased the legal framework for businesses and SMEs can be registered online, there is still a wide gap between the formulation of rules and their implementation. There is still a widely intransparent, bureaucratic and inefficient legal basis for SMEs which is discouraging the registration of new businesses. With the goal to improve SME competitiveness the government has introduced a variety of support incentives and reduced its direct interference. Export consulting services and other activities have improved the situation. However, there is research evidence that promotional funds and incentives are not available for SMEs. Moreover, import and export quotas are not easily obtained due to high bureaucracy and difficulties to obtain import-export quotas. This opens a demand for a concept such as the Reverse Umbrella Company Concept, where directed help can be provided for SMEs. However, there is also evidence that SMEs sometimes are detained by the quota regulations and have to register as subcontractors for larger firms and state owned enterprises (SOEs). (CIA, 2012; Runckel, 2011; World Bank, 2012; Nguyen et al, 2009) All in all, several studies and current economic involutions reveal a positive development of Vietnamese economy and the openness for reforms. However, there is a huge gap between the written legal basis and the real state of the economy. SMEs lack support and are in a disadvantageous position compared to SOEs.

Culture

Family is very important to Vietnamese. Often three generations life together in one house or work in the same family owned business. Thereby, hierarchy is very important when living together in family and society.

Naturally, the father is the head of the family and the bread winner. Generally, older people are considered wise and experienced.

Typically, for many Asian cultures the notion of face is deeply anchored in the society and business culture. Individuals, groups as well as companies have face and direct their actions towards preserving it in all situations. Thereby, face can be described as person's dignity, prestige and reputation, however there is much more to this concept. This influences society as well as business tremendously. Business relationships tend to be rather formal and distanced. Vietnamese feel the need to establish a relationship before conducting business and are therefore rather long term oriented. This sometimes slows down decision making. The spoken word is more important than in Western cultures, hence promises should be only made if they can be kept. (CIA World Factbook, 2012; Communicaid Group Ltd., 2009; Kwintessential, 2012, Nguyen, 2009)

Hypothesis 7: The differences in culture, especially business culture, between Vietnamese and Swiss or other European nations pose a significant barrier to internationalization.

All of these facts should be kept in mind when developing and implementing the Reverse Umbrella Company Concept. Many of the mentioned issues will play a role while working with a Vietnamese SME and agreeing on the concrete action plan for the internationalization. Probably, the notion of face is the least obvious, but has the most severe impact on decision making and other critical factors. As soon as the Vietnamese counterpart faces any risk, be it business or private life, he/she will weight any decision against the likeliness of losing face in front of others and most likely not take a risk. Therefore, it will be key to provide calculable risks and minimize uncertainty in the eyes of the business partner.

3.6. Conceptual Framework

The literature review has provided various concepts and theories that have earned attention and recognition in the theoretical and practical world. In order to use them for this research, they have to be grouped and related to each other. Figure 7 shows an attempt of developing a framework this research will be conducted within. The basis for this framework is the decision to internationalize. Assuming that this decision is positive the basic goal is to overcome all barriers and enter the target market. Thereby, within the home country an SME faces several factors that influence its decisions and actions. Such factors are the prevailing culture of the home country, the internal barriers that are posed by the country as well as by the SME itself and networks the SME is member of. Those networks can exist within the country and consist of business partners, associations and others, but can be an external institution (e.g. the RUCC) as well and be established throughout the process.

To overcome the existing internal and external barriers two basic theoretical approaches are considered within this framework. The first is described by the stage theory, following a step by step approach. The second is an alternative process that is powered by other factors and the avoidance of common internationalization barriers.

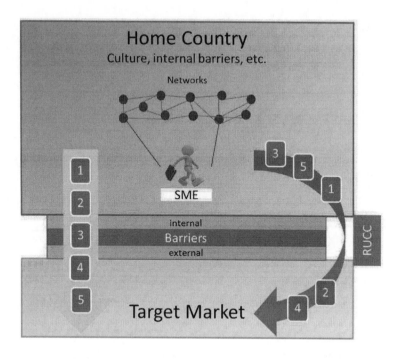

Figure 7 Conceptual Framework RUCC

As already mentioned, a SMEs decision making process of whether and how to internationalize is very complex. Research revealed that, among others, three major factors play a role during this process. All of them are interrelated and ought to be brought into relation. The first factor is the amount of risk the SME is willing to bear with the decision to internationalize. This can imply any kid of risk as subjectively perceived by the individual SME. For instance, this can be the risk of "loosing face" or the risk of jeopardizing the business. The second factor is the amount of control the SME has over its own business in terms of operations, decision making et al. The third factor is the amount of resources the SME is willing or able to invest into the internationalization process. These can be financial resources as well as human capital, cognitive resources or anything that is of value to the company. All of these factors act together and impact decision processes prior to the internationalization as well as the internationalization process itself. Generally, the relationship of these three factors can be simplified as in figure 8. The higher the resource commitment of the SME is, the more risky the operations automatically become, because simply more is at stake for the company. However, this also increases the control over decisions and actions, because the SME can choose between different options and take different directions. With other words, control increases freedom and flexibility during the internationalization process. A practical example could be given using the involvement of third parties in the process. If an SME invests more resources into the internationalization it might be able to avoid partnering with another SME or sharing the profit with a consultant. It would further have more control over how to handle things and how to reach its goals. However, this would also mean that the SME is taking more risk, because it can rely on less help as opposed to partnering with another firm.

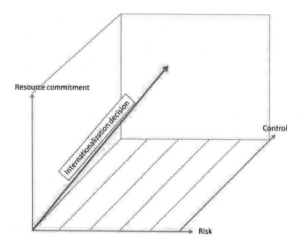

Figure 8 3D Model: Relationship of Risk, Control and Resource Commitment during Internationalization

During the internationalization all of those factors have to be balanced and evaluated by the respective SME in order to reach a passable way of reaching the goal. Logically, this balance is a highly individual and subjective state involving the influence of various soft factors, such as the personality of the CEO. Therefore, is ought to be evaluated how the RUCC will be impacted by this insight.

Hypothesis 8: The choices and decisions of SMEs during internationalization are highly influenced by the relationship of resource commitment, control over the own operations and perception of risk.

4. Market analysis

Every company that is to use the RUCC has to go through several stages. Besides, stages such as the first consulting event, a market analysis serves as the basis for the planning and implementation of the RUCC.

The goal of this chapter is the determination and estimation of practicability regarding the Reverse Umbrella Company Concept. Hereunto, a general model for the basic calculation will be formed and tested using the example of Vietnamese Trung Kien and its export to the Swiss market. Thereby, the basic idea of Terpstra and Sarathy (2000) will be followed. According to them the criteria for evaluating foreign market entry methods depends on the answer to two questions: firstly, how well can the entrant market its services through any particular entry strategy and secondly what are the benefits and costs of the different strategies. This chapter ought to show how the Reverse Umbrella Company Concept could work in practice and add to the revelation of its advantages and disadvantages.

For introducing the overall framework and case of Trung Kien and building upon it the following chapter is divided into four parts.

4.1. Vietnamese Trung Kien

In order to get a brief sense of the market analysis and practical relation, the author has decided to provide an overview of Trung Kien.

The company Trung Kien is named after its owner and is a Vietnamese SME with approximately 22 employees. Trung Kien is a family owned business in the packaging industry and specializes on all kinds of bags, preferably for the cement industry. Moreover, the company already cooperates with established brand, such as Holcim, on the Vietnamese market. The goal of the company is to go beyond the Vietnamese market with the help of the Reverse Umbrella Company Concept.

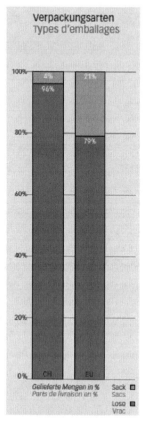

Figure 9 Packaging of cement - comparison Switzerland and EU (Source: CemSuisse, 2012)

4.2. The Swiss Cement Market

Cement is everywhere. It is the most important building and construction component and the basis for all development and advancement of a society. Switzerland is one of the view self-sustaining countries in the world when it comes to cement production since the basic components chalk and clay are easily available. The world's largest cement producer Holcim is an inherently Swiss company. Moreover, Swiss cement producers are leading in energy efficiency and innovation. Especially, the fact that cement production is an energy and resource intensive industry accounts for the long term orientation and innovative pressure of the whole industry. The long term orientation is a very distinctive feature for the cement industry worldwide. In 2011 Switzerland had a consumption of 4.68 million tons of cement. With an average annual growth rate of approximately 3% since 1998 the demand for cement was constantly growing. However, according to

CemSuisse it has slowed down in recent years. Switzerland produces approximately 25 different sorts of cement including CEM1 and CEM2 that account for 98% of the market demand. Importantly, cement production is considered a heavy CO_2 inefficient industry which is why the Swiss cement industry is investing in R&D on a large scale. Figure 9 shows how differently cement is being sold in Switzerland and the EU: whereas in Switzerland only 4% of the cement is packaged in bags, in the EU in average 21% of the cement is sold in bags. (CemSuisse, 2012; Verband der Schweizerischen Cementindustrie, 2012, BFS, 2012)

4.3. Estimations of Market Potential

After having provided the basic information needed to classify the situation, the market analysis proceeds with the estimations needed to calculate the application of the Reverse Umbrella Company Concept.

The estimation of production, sales and other business development indicators is very individual respective to the industry and product. Therefore, at this point no universal model for the calculation of different variables is provided.

For the planning and calculation of the RUCC several variables have to be estimated. The goal is to determine the market potential for the products of any company that is to use the RUCC. In order to do so, it is essential to get an idea about the current production capacity and to estimate the potential sales in the target market.

The access to information about production capacities of Trung Kien is fairly limited. Therefore, at this point we assume that Trung Kien has two (based on the size and operating personnel) fully functional production lines. Further, it is probable that these production lines are not state of the art technology since we are speaking of a Vietnamese SME. Hence, as an estimation basis serves a 1985 Newlong production line for packaging materials. The following link provides a buying opportunity for such a machine including all technical criteria: http://www.bohemia-grafia.de/de/maschinen/verpackung/papier-verpack/schlauch/000962-komplett-zementsack-herstellungslinie-newlong According to the dataset, the maximal output of this machine is 160 bags per minute, when working under full capacity. We estimate that both lines are working at a 70% capacity level for 270 days annually. That includes the consideration of working days only, maintenance of the machines, a 10 hour shift and other factors that might impact production. This estimation might be unrealistic, however at this point the estimation will have no influence on the processes of the overall concept and the step by step approximation to goal. Therefore, we can estimate the current production capacity: 2 production lines with 160 bags/minute at 10 hours/day and 270 days/year with a capacity level of 70% = 36.288.000 bags per year. Further, we can assume that only 20% of the production can be exported since the rest is being sold to existing clients in Vietnam. The acquisition of new production lines is not considered since the internationalization will be very resource intensive. Consequently, the **estimated production volume** of bags that can be exported to Switzerland is **7.257.600 bags**.

Now it is due to estimate the potential sales of the production on the Swiss market. Serving as the basis are the 4,68 million tons of cement produced in Switzerland. Since only 4% is packaged in bags, the relevant market volume is 187.200 tons of cement. (CemSuisse, 2012) Assuming that all by

Trung Kien produced bags have a volume of 25kg that would result in an estimated **demand of 7.488.000 25kg** bags for the Swiss market.

On the one hand, the basic conclusion would be that the demand can be easily covered. On the other hand, it could be assumed that Trung Kien won't penetrate 100% of the market and that Swiss cement producers already have covered their supply of packaging materials. However, it could be a starting point and a way to find access to the European market. For instance, neighboring Germany has an annual production of roughly 28 million tons with a larger part packaged in bags (Lafarge, 2012). Moreover, bags made out of different materials are needed in various industries. Hence, this analysis could be expanded and elaborated. However, at this point it is important to stress that this analysis serves as an example solely. The goal is to explain the basic steps of how to approach the RUCC using Trung Kien as a practical example.

4.4. Competitor Analysis

Now that the theoretical potential has been estimated, a major point would be the competitor analysis with the goal to estimate the realistic market potential and determine how difficult it would be to penetrate the market, reach this potential and hold or expand it. In order to do so, an analysis of the competitors has to be made. Depending on product, industry and goal this analysis can be executed using various tools and techniques, such as Porter's Five Forces, SWOT and USP Analysis.

For instance, Porter's Five Forces help a business to analyze and understand the strength of the current competitive position. It consists of five components:

1. Supplier Power: how easy is it for your suppliers to drive up prices for the goods you use to produce your product?

2. Buyer Power: how easy is it for your customers to drive down prices?

3. Threat of Substitution: how easy and fast is it for your customers to replace you with another supplier?

4. Threat of New Entry: how easy and fast can new competitors enter the same market and compete with you for the same customers?

5. Competitive Rivalry: what is the number of your competitors and what are they capable of? How can they threaten your market position or USP?

Appendix 4 shows how these forces play together and draws an overall picture. It creates a good sense of the whole industry a business is in and explains the correlation of various factors. (Mindtools, 2012)

Applying this to Trung Kien in a superficial way could result in the following:

Threat of New Entry:
o Not expensive to enter the industry
o Cost advantages difficult to reach
o Barriers in Switzerland high
o Low tech

Threat of New Entry

Buyer Power:
o Number of customers low
o Order sizes large
o Ability to substitute high
o Costs of changing supplier low

Supplier Power (+)

Competitive Rivalry
o Many internat. competitors combined with low customer loyalty

Buyer Power

Supplier Power (in Vietnam):
o Many suppliers with various sizes
o Low-tech supply
o Easy to substitute

Threat of Substitution

Threat of Substitution:
o Cost of change very low
o Standardized product
o Many competitors

Figure 10 Application of Porter's Five Forces towards Trung Kien

Summing up the analysis, the position of Trung Kien on the Swiss market would be rather difficult. The threat of substitution and buyer power are very high and potential competitors can be found everywhere in the world since this product is easy to produce and can be produced cheaper through scale. However, the major advantage of Trung Kien is the eased access to the Swiss market through the RUCC and the price. Looking at labor costs in Vietnam, the expertise through specialization on this product and the already existing partnerships with Holcim on the Vietnamese market, Trung Kien is likely to be successfully marketing its products in Switzerland.

5. Findings

The following chapter represents all research findings clustering them into 7 sections. Purposefully, some of the information could be repeatedly mentioned in differing contexts to provide the overall picture or serve the purpose of relating and connecting it.

5.1. General Opinion

This section presents the findings regarding the general attitude and opinion of the participants when asked about internationalization and import/export promotion. Generally, all three participants expressed a highly positive attitude towards internationalization. However, two participants where solely positive pointing out the mutual benefits of companies and markets on both sides, whereas one participant expressed concern about the possibility to endanger local companies by creating artificial competition on home market and weaken its position globally.

Two participants agreed that it is quite hard to fight globalization and the strong influence it has had and will have in the future. Since barely no company has not been influenced by global economic developments, it is perceived as a question of survival and therefore a must to internationalize the own operations or at least think in global terms. In terms of promoting internationalization candidates all mentioned the fact that governmental agencies stop at a certain point and further more advanced services which would provide assistance for SMEs are missing. One expert points out in that context that developing an idea similar to that of the RUCC is the logical consequence of this deficit.

5.2. Comparison of Company Structure

This section is designed to provide an impression of how the three experts perceive differences between European (in particular Swiss) and Asian (in particular Vietnamese) SMEs. In the interview guide this section relates to question 1 and 5 respectively.

Generally, all interviewees agree that there are definite differences in quality, innovativeness and pricing of products. Regarding the structure of SMEs opinions are quite different: from the perspective of the Asian expert companies in Vietnam and Europe are quite similar in terms of structure. One interviewee mentions that quite many companies in Vietnam have Chinese owners and are therefore more advanced in terms of professionalizing and modernizing their businesses. However, the third interviewee is convinced that differences in structures, such as the management, can vary enormously. Nevertheless, all experts point out the special importance of family businesses in developing countries and especially Vietnam.

Regarding the readiness to internationalize through export all experts agree that the full potential companies on both sides has not been reached yet. However, in developing countries there is a strong tendency for promoting internationalization and even stronger strive to promote local trade and internationalization to geographically close countries.

All experts associate attributes such as quality, innovativeness, advancement, business excellence, but also high prices rather with European companies mentioning that SMEs in developing economies often have deficits in these areas. However, all experts agree that those differences are diminishing rapidly and it is increasingly hard to make a clear distinction. The difference in prices of products produced is a clear difference mentioned by every expert. However, there is a discrepancy of awareness regarding the lingual and cultural differences: the two western experts both mention the fact that lingual and cultural sensibility and the ability to communicate with foreigners are poor in SMEs from developing countries such as Vietnam. In contrary, the Vietnamese expert does not mention this difference at any point.

One expert points out that European and in particular Swiss SMEs are rather slow in their decision making process since they are very security oriented, whereas SMEs in Vietnam are rather growth oriented and therefore willing to take risk. Another interviewee highlights that Asian SMEs often lack the skills to market their products effectively and experience huge difficulties with the transformation of contacts and opportunities into closed deals.

All in all, the central differences mentioned by the experts are the fulfillment of quality requirements, norms and standards and the pricing of products.

5.3. Comparison of Markets

This section ought to reflect how Western and in particular the Swiss and developing country markets (in particular the Vietnamese) differ in indicators such as competitiveness, growth, saturation and demand. With respect to the interview guide it particularly relates to question 2 and 5.

All participants point out quality and innovativeness as key distinguishing factors between western and developing markets. Moreover, the term "quality" is being mentioned over and over again throughout whole two interviews. Further, all participants agree that products can be produced to quite lower prices in e.g. Vietnam as similar products in Europe and that most SMEs still use this fact as a central USP and strategy to enter the European market. But, from the point of view of the two Western exerts this advantage is diminishing as prices for raw materials are globalized and large corporations can afford to reduce prices to a minimum through economies of scale. Hence, the major reason that two interviewees attribute to the lower production costs is the cheap labor in developing economies. One interviewee believes R&D expenditures in developing economies are growing and that quality differences are being constantly reduced. In this context one participant places the example of the agricultural sector where Asian companies have had to answer the quality, hygiene and safety regulations of the EU regarding shrimp production. Nowadays various Asian countries produce shrimps for the European market answering all quality standards and conforming to all regulations. Two participants agree that technological innovations and quality will be growing in developing economies. One of them even goes further by making an example of the software industry and stating that differences in this sector are minimal. One interviewee mentions that the decision of going to Europe for selling the product to higher prices as compared to internationalizing to geographically close country becomes slowly outdated. The reason is that regarding many products prices in Europe and for instance Asia are similarly high. As a result, companies don't need to make the effort internationalizing to Europe and often chose a close and less regulated country for their export. One expert explicitly mentions that local trade agreements and the promotion of internationalization to geographically close markets are growing and that trade will increase rapidly on for instance the inner Asia market. Moreover, one participant addresses the differences in economic regulations and the legal basis. The expert points out that payment conditions can vary enormously: in certain European countries payments for delivered goods can be made after 120 days (e.g. Italy), whereas in developing economies payment terms are usually tighter.

All in all, differences in quality of production and regulations, norms, standards et al. are the central scheme of this question. However, all participants believe that differences are diminishing and making a categorical / imprudent classification would be rather inaccurate.

5.4. Internationalization Process

5.4.1. Requirements

This section represents the findings relating to the question of which requirements an SMEs from a developing country and in particularly Vietnam has to fulfill to be able to internationalize its operations successfully. This includes answers to the questions 3, 4 and 5 from the interview guide.

All experts agree that the first and most basic requirement is the ability of the SME to produce a product that is demanded on the target market and qualitatively sufficient enough to be bought there. The second requirement that has been mentioned by two interviewees is trust. This relates to trust in the ability to internationalize, trust in the partners that provide assistance and advice during the internationalization process and trust within the company itself. One interviewee points out that especially for Asian countries trust is a very important reoccurring notion. Another participant confirms that especially from the point of view of European buyers building trust is an important goal since many European companies are skeptical of suppliers from developing countries which can harm the seller-buyer relationship.

Further, all interviewees mention the cultural and lingual requirements that ought to be fulfilled in order to establish business relationships between companies across borders. Thereby, the notion of culture is perceived as an internal requirement by one participant, too. This means that the company culture has to be clearly growth and internationalization focus. Moreover, the company has to be able to think in an international context. Two participants mention the commitment and goal to internationalize as an important requirement. Nevertheless, the Asian expert perspective represents a weakened estimation regarding the necessity of being able to deal with foreign culture and language.

Importantly, out of two experts that promote internationalization to Europe from a European perspective one says that the fulfillment of the requirements mentioned above is the responsibly of the SME, whereas the other expert argues that intermediaries can help the SME to fulfill these requirements, which however demands a higher level of trust.

Another often mentioned requirement is the fulfillment of regulations, standards and rules in the target country and the knowledge and awareness of those legal aspects. Regarding this requirement all participants have a similar opinion.

From the financial perspective the basic idea is similar among all participants: the demand has to be sufficient enough be able to sell the product and generate a profit that would at least cover the costs and generate a break-even within 2-3 years. One expert is precise and states that the market potential ought to be able to generate a return of 2 million Euros per year in order to cover the costs of internationalization. However, all experts agree that the concrete calculation can vary significantly and is highly dependent upon many factors such as the concrete product, market potential and achievable margin.

5.4.2. Barriers

For this section the primary source was question 6 of the interview guide. However, the participants came up with thoughts regarding barriers throughout the whole course of the interview which is why this section will explicitly sum up all the barriers mentioned. Logically, certain barriers will repeat the content of other sections within the findings chapter. All barriers mentioned by the interviewees are summed up in figure 11.

Barrier	Description	Expert 1	Expert 2	Expert 3
Quality	Quality regulations in the target market and quality of products produced	X	X	X
Language	Not speaking the language of the target country or English	X	X	
Culture	Company culture and cultural differences (e.g. business culture)	X	X	
Legal	Legal barriers such as	X	X	X

	regulations, norms, standards, compliance issues			
Capital	Capital requirements to internationalize	X	X	X
Mindset	Perspective and mindset of management	X	X	
Trust	Trust (with outside partners and inside the company)	X		X
Reputatio n	Reputation of the country, the SME is from, in Europe		X	

Figure 11 Barriers on internationalization of Asian SMEs

Clearly, the necessity to answer quality requirements, legal norms and standards was one of the most frequently mentioned barrier in all interviews. Also the problem to raise money for the resource intensive process is a fact that every interviewee has in mind when asked about the obstacles of internationalization. The other barriers in the table are mentioned by the experts quite often. However, only one expert comes up with the thought that the reputation of the country is a quite significant factor.

5.4.3. Relationship between risk, control and resource commitment

Resulting from the literature review the relationship between risk, control over the own company and resource commitment of the company appeared to be an important notion for internationalization from the point of view of the SME wishing to internationalize. In the interview the participants were explicitly asked for their opinion about the relationship of these three factors whenever appropriate. The results are presented in the section below. More information in the idea of this relationship can be found in the **conceptual framework.**

Generally, all interviewees agree that the decision to internationalize bears a high risk potential. Thereby, the risk is seen from a financial and resource perspective meaning that building up a foreign subsidiary can be a very costly process which comes along with the possibility not to pay off in the end. But at the same time personnel and internal company resources such as machines are being oriented towards the internationalization which can have negative effects on domestic operations. Two participants mention this in their answers. Risk is also perceived in a cultural context. Especially in Asian cultures the risk of "loosing face" is avoided and perceived as highly threatening which in turn has certain effect on decision making and risk taking. One interviewee, when asked about internationalization methods, mentions that direct export presents the highest amount of control over the own operations to a company, but at the same time bear the highest amount of risk. Two interviewees represent the thought that an initial spending prior to the internationalization for e.g. the participation on affair or an market analysis represents a big hurdle for an SME in developing countries and that most SMEs are not willing to take this risk. The point of view of the third participant supports this idea from a different point of view, the opinion that this initial spending is a high risk because of the uncertainty of the outcome. However, all experts agree that the loss of control over the own operations and decision making is perceived as highly risky as well. From their experience companies are not willing to give away control. Nevertheless, two interviewees see a balance between risk and control: they argue that by giving away control a company can reduce the risk it takes and therefore can balance these factors. All interviewees agree that the more intermediaries are included into the internationalization process them more control is being lost over decisions.

The commitment with the own resources is highly important for two participants. They both agree that an initial spending is a high barrier for every SME wishing to participate in an export promotion program. Hence, on the one side companies that might be potentially suitable, but don't take the risk are excluded. On the other side the interviewees argue that companies with a clear goal are more committed and have realistic expectations about their potential. Therefore, they perceive this initial spending as a calculable risk which they are willing to take more likely.

All in all, the interviewees see a clear connection of these three factors and a relation to the process of internationalization.

5.4.4. Vietnamese Peculiarities

Vietnam is being perceived as a fast growing country with a huge potential, but a lot of deficits by all participants. Especially, the need for trust and personal relationships is a reoccurring argument in two interviewees. One expert argues that there is a deficit in thinking in networks and connecting businesses with a common goal as it is being done in Europe. Two European experts are aware of the cultural peculiarities in Vietnam and attribute them with a high importance for the internationalization. In contrary the Vietnamese perspective suggest that culture does not play a very important role and does not pose a high barrier to internationalization.

5.5. RUCC (9)

5.5.1. Opinion about the RUCC on the basis of the UCC

This findings section is one of the central towards answering the grand tour research question. Since all experts were familiar with the Umbrella Company Concept or have been made familiar with its principle in the course of the interview they all had the opportunity make suggestions about how to make it work as a reverse principle supporting the internationalization of Vietnamese SME to Europe. However, the findings in this section alone are not ought to answer the research question completely.

One expert believes than the idea of a Reverse Umbrella Company Concept is the logical step resulting from the deficit of such promotion programs on a corporate level. The participant argues that this novel concept has the ability to unite the advantages of direct and indirect export as the major alternatives to the RUCC. At the same time typical disadvantages of export such as high risk or financial effort are eliminated. Going on, the expert mentions that in its basis the RUCC could represent a direct export model with a primary sales responsible, but without the costs for infrastructure and administration. However, there are a lot of alternative internationalization models that are not covered in literature, but being tested. In this context the participant argues that more research has to be conducted on success factors that can be critical to internationalize with the help of alternative approaches such as the RUCC.

One expert highlights the importance of choosing the right SMEs that would be suitable for the European market in terms of products and goals. Hereby, the idea to cluster companies is clearly a favorable approach. The goal of such a concept should be the direct connection of seller and buyer and the establishment of stable long term oriented contract between those two. At the same time, this expert argues that import promotion through such a concept should pose no threat to local producers in the target market and not create competition artificially. All in all, the experts speak positive about the basic idea behind the RUCC and express only one central issue: the prospective profitability of allocating one sales person to each SME and the problem of covering this enormous cost with the return an SME can realize on a European market.

5.5.2. Advantages

This section discusses the findings related to advantages of RUCC concept and its basic idea and relates to the questions 9 and 10, but considers information from the whole three interviews.

The two advantages mentioned by all interviewees are the access to networks in Europe and the limited risk. The participants argue that the access to contacts and is a central advantage because it eases the finding of new buyers and participating SMEs can profit from the availability of certain information that is crucial for operating their business on a foreign market. One interviewee mentions the overall supportive function these networks can obtain and their importance for the internationalization process. Regarding risk, all experts agree that that it is being reduced for each individual SME and that the risk of failing is way lower since the RUCC providing company is interested in the SME to succeed and therefore is providing a maximum amount of support.

Another advantage mentioned by two interviewees is the eased financial situation from the perspective of SME. The costs are about one third of what building up a foreign subsidiary would take. Further, the speed of entering the foreign market is significantly increased as one participant argues. Certainly, the same is valid for the exiting the market since all activities on the market are formalized through a contract which can be legally terminated by one of the two parties. These advantages increase the flexibility of the company and enable the SME to concentrate on its core business and the export without wasting resources for other things. In this context, two interviewees mention the reduction of bureaucratic hurdles and the simplification of the internationalization process for the SME as one of the major advantages. This advantage is seen both sided: on the hand the bureaucracy in the target country can be overcome, on the other hand the bureaucratic systems of many developing countries can be bridged, thereby creating an advantage for the buyer, too.

One interviewee points out the emphasis the RUCC places on relationships and networks as one of the major advantages. The provision of a sales person that is directly responsible for one SME is a favorable scenario, especially when having products with a high need of explanation.

From the perspective of a Swiss company buying products from overseas the RUCC can offer the advantage of creating additional security. Especially, the development of a SPOC (single point of contact) concept where the buyer can process everything with one company is an "extreme" advantage.

5.5.3. Disadvantages

This section illustrates the finding regarding the weaknesses and disadvantages of the RUCC as perceived by the experts. It particularly relates to questions 9 and 10 of the interview guide.

Among the disadvantages mentioned by all experts are high dependency of the SME on the RUCC and the sales person working for it. In this regards the access to the sales person is fairly limited through geographical, lingual and cultural differences. Further, the whole concept relies on the success of the sales person and its ability to sell the product, as the participants argue. Such a high dependency on one person elevates the risk and endangers the success of the internationalization attempt. As a result, the need to find a sophisticated sales person with broad networks, a good track record and the acceptance to work for an unknown company with low reputation whatsoever instead of working for a global player is central.

Another issue addressed by one interviewee is the market appearance of the SME in the target country. The question whether the products can be effectively branded or whether they would be sold under one joint RUCC logo is highly important and concerns the expert. If the brand can be build up only after leaving the RUCC this could be regarded a major disadvantage.

A similar concern is expressed by another expert. The question of "who is writing the bill" is of central importance. This means that if the product is produced by one company and sold by another (the RUCC) the buyer would perceive it as dealing with an intermediary and assume that an additional margin is placed on the products. Further, the payment process would be less clear and by far more risky. The expert considers this as one of the soft success factors of the RUCC.

5.5.4. Cost Structure

When asked about concrete estimations or financial evaluations regarding the RUCC participants were rather reserved. All of them reasoned that the concrete financial model will strictly depend on the SME, its products and the data revealed by a detailed market analysis.

However, two interviewees stated that within the RUCC the sales person is a critical value. In any European market, especially the Swiss, the costs for a profound and experienced sales person will be high. If not subsidized by the RUCC the SME would have to cover this cost and the costs for the initial market analysis and coaching. As a result enough return would have to be generated in the target market to cover these costs and eventually break-even within 2-3 years. One interviewee states in this connection that the market potential of a single SME should be at least 2 million Euros per year. Further, the interviewee makes clear that no incentive is ought to be paid to the RUCC. Payments to the RUCC would be covering the market analysis and initial as well as ongoing support activities only. Certainly, the sales person would be provided with a success oriented payment model.

In this context, on interviewee highlight the importance of the payment and legal scheme. The experts argues that a SPOC scheme where the buyer would have to deal with one company as seller and invoicing party only would be highly advantageous. From the point of view of Swiss companies a minimal difference in price would be sufficient enough to buy the products, but only in case that a Swiss buyer will face no disadvantages, discomfort due to additional margins of an intermediary or effort to take care of the customs and taxing. The expert points out that this factor can be a highly important advantage which can give be the final trigger to sing a contract.

In a nutshell, two very important things were mentioned by the participants. First, the question of whether the high costs for the initial market analysis and recruitment of the sales person can be covered and whether ongoing costs for the sales person and RUCC services can be covered by the turnover of the SME and eventually be transformed into a profitable scheme. Second, the way of how the trade process will be designed legally and the question of how "comfortable" it is for the buyer.

5.6. Support

This section represents the findings regarding the support that is necessary for a Vietnamese SME wanting to internationalize with the help of the RUCC. It includes information collected from every part of the interviews, but relates to question 7 of the interview guide in particularly.

Two interviewees argue that only companies that fulfill the requirements should be even considered for this promotion activity in the first place. However, after asked how to evaluate the suitability of an SME opinions were quite different. One interviewee argues that the only SMEs that are willing to make the first investment for a market analysis or another concrete supportive action should be considered, because they are likelier to have the certain mindset and motivation needed to succeed. In contrary, another interviewee argues that SMEs ought to be selected according to the quality and prospective success of their products.

As a second step, all interviewees agree that assistance with a market analysis is necessary. Should the market analysis reveal a positive scenario for the SME all interviewees argue that knowledge about the target market, its peculiarities such as regulations and norms that concern the product and further legal aspects is crucial. Further, the opinions separate again: one participant argues that the support should go as far as providing a whole marketing concept and business development plan for the SME and consistently assist the SME over a period of 1-2 years. Thereby, even the right execution of the sales pipeline should be supported. Logically, the RUCC should be in a permanent consulting position.

Another interviewee is in favor of a maximum commitment of the SME to its own internationalization. This should be done by providing knowledge rather than operative assistance. The expert argues that workshops and the close relation of the SME with the sales person would be most helpful. However, the first steps into the target country ought to be supported more intensively through actions such as the assistance during negotiations with buyers.

All in all, the experts are certain that support should exceed formal organization of the internationalization in administrative terms and offer a variable amount of support.

5.7. Future Outlook

In this section the answers from question 11 regarding the perspective and future of the RUCC concept are summed up.

All experts believe that alternative internationalization models will have a good chance of becoming used more widely and can present a sophisticated alternative to the classical models of internationalization. Especially, all interviewees make clear that models targeting SMEs are rather rare and there is a deficit of internationalization promotion on a corporate level. Two participants mention the need to efficiently marketing novel models and promoting their use across borders in order to gain recognition. One participant argues that Asian SMEs are developing very fast and models such as the RUCC will be needed to answer the demand for international growth within developing economies. However, one participant is not solely optimistic and argues that alternative promotion channels such as the internet or fairs are not necessarily in need of this type of model.

All in all, the sentiment is rather positive, however not euphoric.

6. Discussion and Analysis

This research has proved that novel supportive internationalization concepts for SMEs such as the RUCC are needed. All experts have agreed that these kinds of concepts will have a future as alternative approaches. Not all participants agreed that especially SMEs are in need of a novel concept, however the findings support hypothesis 3[3] and thereby justify the evolvement of the RUCC.

6.1. Basis for Internationalization

The research has shown that experts generally agree on the differences between markets and companies. The greatest distinctions can be attributed to differences in quality, amount of regulations and the sophistication of norms, certifications and rules. Not to forget are the cultural peculiarities of each country and the language barrier. For the experts it was rather hard to determine what basis an SME should have to make successful use of the RUCC concept. As the conceptual framework makes clear that every SME represents the business culture and peculiarities of its home country, the basis should be the evaluation of these peculiarities, including legal aspects and soft factors and their confrontation with the goals of the SME and the target country's characteristics. In the particular case of this research a Vietnamese SME must have a clear internationalization goal and obtain the ability to think in international terms. The SME should possess the ability to raise awareness of cultural differences and adapt its business culture to the Swiss market.

Certainly, the SME has to be offering a competitive product to a reasonable price with a rather high market potential in the Swiss market. To make further use of the RUCC a trust basis has to be created. Thereby, personal relationships and the procurement of security will play an important role considering the characteristics of Vietnamese culture.

---

[3] A list with all hypothesis can be found in the appendix

This research could not clearly determine what the ultimate basis for a Vietnamese SME internationalizing to Switzerland would be and where the RUCC should step in. However, the minimal basis is the selection of SMEs with a strong product with potential on the Swiss market and the clear determination and mindset to internationalize.

6.2. Support through the RUCC

6.2.1. Overcoming barriers

The barriers to internationalization are the basic reason why concepts such as the RUCC are demanded. From the barriers presented in figure 11 of the findings section all appear to be important and have been confirmed by prior research mentioned in the literature review section. However, the special importance of overcoming internal barriers and the underestimation of this fact, as stated by hypothesis 2, could be supported through this research. This is coherent to the findings of Leonidou (2004) and an OECD-APEC study in 2006. Generally, all experts showed recognition of internal barriers, but the importance attributed to their significance for the success of internationalization was quite different. Especially, cultural and lingual barriers showed low recognition by the Vietnamese expert. Therefore, the results of this research can only partly support hypothesis 7. Nevertheless, two experts were aware of the cultural and lingual barriers and supported this notion. The results create the impression that obvious barriers are considered more and with a higher intensity, whereas the overcoming the cultural barrier can be crucial to the success of an internationalization attempt. Hence, the RUCC concept has to take into consideration internal barriers as well, as visualized by the conceptual framework. In this regards the RUCC could provide assistance and coaching with aspect of business culture and recommend language classes. Importantly, the collected knowledge about Vietnamese culture, especially the notion of face, have shown that finding the right solution does not mean to have found the right approach. The general lesson is providing a flexible consulting method that can be adjusted to various situations and needs.

Hypothesis 4 could only be partly supported, too. The absence of strategic thinking and planning, limited scale of operations and restricted access to experts is and skilled personnel are only partly mentioned. One expert inexplicitly mentions that SMEs that are too small will not be able to execute international operations and perform effectively on sales which could be attributed to the aspect of limited scale within the hypothesis. Further, the RUCC indirectly solves the problem of accessing experts and skilled personnel through its network and recruiting services. However, these aspects need to be researched more explicitly and developed fitting the RUCC.

Regarding the amount and extent of support for an SME prior to and during the internationalization the thoughts are quite different. This is also a result of very different experiences with various companies in many industries. The logical consequence is the development of a flexible support scheme where the amount and kind of support could be adopted towards the needs of each SME individually. Hypothesis 5 suggests a broad generalization stating that all Vietnamese SMEs demand extensive support to internationalize to a Western market. Considering that every expert mentioned how differently SMEs are prepared for internationalization and how differences between Asian and European companies are diminishing, hypothesis 5 can't be supported. This creates the difficulty of evaluating each SME individually, but at the same time supports the necessity to provide flexible amounts of consulting through the RUCC.

The question this research can't provide an answer to, is how far the RUCC involvement should go and whether the RUCC should provide operational assistance to the SMEs by supporting them in marketing and sales issues. A possible solution would be to provide help on demand to the point of the first contract, sales agreement or similar.

6.2.2. Risk, Control and Resource Commitment

On the basis of the literature review the conceptual framework provided an approach of how the three factors could be correlated. In addition, data from the interviews reveals that this concept obtains certain significance for the RUCC. Generally, the evaluation of these criteria from the perspective of an SME can help determining the demand for support and predict choices the SME will make from a rational perspective. As the cultural research revealed, the need of security and uncertainty avoidance in Vietnam creates a special interest for security. At the same time, the family character of many small and medium sized businesses in Vietnam is likely to demand the maintenance of control over decision making and operations. Additionally, it is clear that initial investments for internationalization to Switzerland are very high and even higher from the perspective of a Vietnamese SME. Connecting all of the mentioned above, the relationship between the three factors could be explained by figure 8: Higher resource commitment means that more control is kept over the own operations and decision making, but requires taking higher risk in terms of financial and intellectual risk. Vietnamese SMEs demand a maximum control of their operations and decision making, but want to reduce their resource commitment and risk to a minimum answering their economic and cultural needs. In a nutshell, the RUCC can present a sophisticated balancing mechanism for this issue. SMEs would reduce their risk, because of being backed up by the whole construct, but would be able to make decisions confidently and competently. Therefore, hypothesis 6 can be supported talking about a "trade-off between avoiding risk and maintaining high control over the own operations".

All in all, the relationship of the presented three factors is highly important to the RUCC concept in terms of understanding the SME and providing an optimal support approach. Nevertheless, hypothesis 8 can't be completely supported: from the point of view of most experts the risk-control-resource commitment notion is logical and supported. However, to be able to approve this hypothesis finally, a quantitative study of several Vietnamese SMEs going through the internationalization process would be necessary.

6.2.3. Networks

The results of the study reveal that making use of networks is one of the bigger advantages the RUCC can offer to SMEs. The possibilities to apply networks throughout the process of internationalization are various. However, the fact that networks are not going to be initially available and will evolve and extended with time of successful RUCC operation needs to be considered. All interviewees agree that networks can play an important role and thereby support hypothesis 1. However, the relationship of networks and internationalization success and their quality to raise confidence of Vietnamese SMEs can't be proven by this research. This factor could be for instance researched in a comprehensive study about the success factors of internationalization concepts.

Nevertheless, the research can reinforce the findings from the literature review ascribing a special relevance of networks to the internationalization of SMEs as opposed to the stage model. This fact is also visualized in the conceptual framework illustrating that internationalization through the RUCC is not passing through traditional stages. One interviewee confirmed that building networks an important initial step from where internationalization can go in any direction. This study confirms that network related approaches such as the RUCC can play an important role during SME internationalization. At the same time, the RUCC concept tackles the lack of formal linkages between businesses in Vietnam as revealed by Thanh Hain Nguyen (2009) by clustering SMEs under one roof and enforcing mutual learning and development.

6.2.4. Market appearance

In the course of the interviews the question of market appearance has been raised as a critical success factor regarding the Swiss market. Results show that Swiss buyers would prefer to get everything from one hand and prefer conduction business with a Swiss company over an Asian. For the RUCC this creates the issue of how to structure the process of exporting and selling the product through the sales person. Additionally, the branding of the products appears to be one distinctive factor that ought to be considered. Unfortunately, the data does not generate a solution for these issues. Most likely, the products will have to be distributed by the RUC and sold by the sales person working for it. An advantage would be the handling of customs and invoicing through the RUC.

6.2.5. Cost Structure

This section should provide an idea of how the RUCC could work in practice using the example of Trung Kien. Based on the estimations in section 4.3 the potential demand of 25kg bags in the Swiss market is 7.488.000 bags. Approaching the goal according to the principle of target costing and assuming that at least a large part of the ongoing costs should be covered and the break-even-point reached in 3 years following calculation is possible:

Initial costs:

CHF 10.000	Market analysis
CHF 20.000	Consulting, coaching, training
CHF 5.000	Recruiting
CHF 10.000	licensing

	Costs		Sales		
	Fixed costs				
	120.000,00 CHF	sales person	7.488.000,00 CHF	overall demand	
	40.000,00 CHF	management fee			
			0,40 CHF	unit price	
	variable costs				
year 1	29.952,00 CHF	customs and taxes	374.400,00 CHF	1st year: realistic potential (5%)	
		(approx. 20% of sales)			
year 2	41.932,80 CHF		524.160,00 CHF	2nd year: realistic potential (7%)	
year 3	59.904,00 CHF		748.800,00 CHF	3rd year: realistic potential (10%)	
	Annual costs		**Turnover (gross)**	**Turnover (net) (15% tax rate)**	**Profit**
year 1	189.952,00 CHF		149.760,00 CHF	127.296,00 CHF	-62.656,00 CHF
year 2	201.932,80 CHF		209.664,00 CHF	178.214,40 CHF	-23.718,40 CHF
year 3	219.904,00 CHF		299.520,00 CHF	254.592,00 CHF	**34.688,00 CHF**

Figure 12 Example Calculation Sheet (original Excel on CD)

This is an example of how the RUCC could work from the financial perspective on a highly simplified level. Following assumptions were made and can be adopted in the Excel table:

- Variable costs are estimated at 20% of the turnover
- 15% business tax is based on the minimal overall business tax in Switzerland (including taxes of the state, cantons and commune)
- A unit price of CHF 0,4 is estimated

According to the calculation the break-even-point will be reached in the third year of operations with a profit of CHF 34.688,00. The first and second year are planned as losses.

6.3. Further Research

All in all, the research has provided valid answers to the research question and sub-questions and contributed to the practical evolvement of the RUCC concept. Moreover, certain results reinforced the information provided in the literature review and could add to it. However, it has also raised many additional questions that need to be researched. Essentially, the following questions are important: how far should the RUCC support an SME and should it intervene in operational activities? How can the immense dependency upon the sales person and its success be reduced or mitigated? How can the sales process and market appearance be structured to reach satisfy Swiss buyers to a maximum? How can risk, control and resource commitment be optimally balanced from the perspective of a SME participating in the RUCC?

Further research could include case studies of one or more companies making use of the RUCC and test the concept in practice. Thereby, empirical research on the success factors of internationalization. In this context, BDO Consultants (2011) mention that numerous studies highlight the challenges faced by SMEs internationalizing, whereas very few provide meaningful comparisons of best practices across economies.

Generally, more research ought to be directed towards SMEs. Cultural and cognitive decision making during internationalization could be examined. Further, more comparative studies on Western and Asian SMEs could lead to insights of how they have to be approached by internationalization models.

7. Conclusion

This research has been conducted in a timely manner as SMEs from developing countries are striving for more growth and lacking opportunities to internationalize their businesses. First and foremost, this research revealed a clear demand for an export promotion model addressing SMEs on a corporate level going beyond the services offered by governmental promotion programs. Participants agree that the comparison of developing countries and Switzerland still reveals many significant differences in terms of quality commitment, innovativeness and sophistication of legal and regulatory basis. Importantly, all experts see these differences shrinking and resist the idea of forejudging based on the country of origin.

The very basis for internationalizing to the Swiss market is considered the availability of a demanded product at a decent quality level and sophisticated price. Using the RUCC an SME should be able to cover a large amount of the ongoing costs and break-even within 3 years to consider the internationalization successful. Beyond these basic requirements, the study revealed that cultural awareness and mindset including the understanding and adaptability towards the Swiss business culture and a clear internationalization goal are desired prerequisites. Resulting from the requirements this research confirmed the importance of raising awareness of barriers to internationalization. In general, all requirements can be considered barriers. However, trust in the own abilities and partners along with the reputation of the home country and capital requirements pose significant hurdles and can only be partially overcome with the help of the RUCC. Nevertheless, the RUCC obtains the ability to provide financial help and other advantages such as increased speed of market entry and exit, risk reduction, flexibility, advisory and coaching services and the overall simplification of the internationalization process. Unfortunately, the high dependency upon the success of a sales person along with the market appearance of the SME were revealed as weaknesses of the RUCC. Further, this study could not determine how far the support offered by the RUCC should go and whether SMEs should be supported on the operational level. Clearly, all experts agreed that SMEs are in need of differing amount of consulting services that address the barriers mentioned above, but also provide marketing, strategy and legal advisory. However, the amount of services needed, has to be flexibly structured to answer the different needs of SMEs.

One interesting notion reinforced by this study, is the relationship of risk, control and resource commitment. It can help explaining decision making and reasoning of SMEs during internationalization addresses the strengths of a concept such as the RUCC.

All in all, the research question could be answered showing which direction is to be taken when adapting the classical Umbrella Company Concept that has been in place for over 12 years to the needs of a Vietnamese SME. Nevertheless, it could not provide a complete and final solution due to the fact that a practical application of the RUCC has not been tested yet and that it revealed several additional issues that need to be solved. Most importantly, the questions of how to structure an SME's market appearance, where to cut the line of support through the RUCC and how to reduce the dependency on one sales person need to be solved through further research.

The answer to these questions and the practical testing of the RUCC will show whether this concept can establish a sustainable alternative for export promotion on a corporate level.

8. List of references

Agarwal, S. and Ramaswami, S.N., 1992. Choice of Foreign Market Entry
Mode: Impact of Ownership, Location and Internationalization
Factors. Journal of International Business Studies Vol. 23, No. 1,
pp.1-27.

Aharoni, Y., 1966. *The Foreign Investment Decision Process*, Boston:
Harvard Graduate School of Business Administration, Division
of Research.

Ahokangas, P., 1998. *Internationalization and resources: an analysis of
processes in Nordic SMSs*. Doctoral dissertation, Vaasa:
University Wasaensis.

Alvarez, R., 2004. *Sources of Export Success in Small- and Medium-sized
Enterprises: The Impact of Public Programs*. International
Business Review, Vol. 13, No. 3, pp. 383-400. Available at:
http://www.sciencedirect.com/science/article/pii/S096959310400
0186 [accessed 21 August 2012].

Andersen, O., 1993. *On the Internationalization Process of Firms: A
Critical Analysis.* Journal of International Business Studies, Vol.
24, No. 2, pp. 209-231.

Andersen, T., 2003. *HRM in SME's – first findings on structure and
practices*. [pdf] Odense M., DK: University of Southern
Denmark. Available at:
http://www.lok.cbs.dk/images/publ/Torben%20Andersen.pdf
[accessed 8 March 2012].

Aristotle, 1982. *The Nicomachean Ethics* (translated by Rackman, H.). London: Harvard University Press.

Atlas.ti, 2011. *The Qualitative Data Analysis & Research Software.* [online] Berlin: Atlas.ti. Available online at: http://www.atlasti.com [accessed 29 January 2012].

Axelsson, B., Johanson, J., 1992. *Foreign market entry – the textbook vs. the network view.* In: Axelsson, B., Easton, E. (Eds.), A New View of Reality, chap. 12.

Bagchi-Sen, S., 1999. *The small and medium sized exporters' problems: An empirical analysis of Canadian manufacturers.* Regional Studies, Vol.33, No.3, pp.231–245.

Bannock, G. and Partners, 1987. *Into Active Exporting.* BOTB Occasional Papers. London: HMSO.

BDO Consultants Pte Ltd, 2011. *Spring Singapore: Study on SME Internationalization Best Practices Across Selected APEC Economies.* [pdf]

Beamish, P. and Lu, J., 2006. *SME Internationalization and Performance: Growth vs. Profitability.* Journal of International Entrepreneurship Vol.4, No.1, pp.27-48. Available at: http://www.springerlink.com/content/v55255674u8m2371/ [accessed 12 October 2012].

Beamish, P. W., 1990. *The Internationalisation Process for Smaller Ontario Firms: A Research Agenda,,* in: Rugman, A. M. (ed.), Research in Global Strategic Management - International

Business Research for the Twenty-First Century: Canada's New
Research Agenda, Greenwich: JAI Press Inc. pp. 77-92.

Bryman, A. and Bell, E., 2011. *Business Research Methods*. 3rd edition.
Oxford: Oxford University Press.

Buckley, J., 1983. *Government-industry relations in exporting: lessons
from the United Kingdom*. In: Czinkota, M., Export Promotion,
the Public and Private Sector Interaction. New York:
Praeger.pp.89-109.

Carson, J., 1993. *A philosophy for marketing education in small firms*.
Journal of Marketing Management. Vol.9, pp.189-204.

Cavusgil, T. and Jacob, N., 1987. *Firm and management characteristics as
discriminators of export marketing activity*. Journal of Business
Research, Vol.15, pp.221–235.

Cavusgil, T., 1980. *On the internationalization process of the firm*.
European Research. Vol.8, No.6, pp.81-273.

Cavusgil, T., 1990. *Export development efforts in the United States:
experiences and lessons learned*. In: Cavusgil, T. and Czinkota,
M. International Perspectives on Trade Promotion and
Assistance. Westport: Quorum Books. Pp. 83-173.

CemSuisse, 2012. *Verband der Schweizerischen Cementindustrie –
Kennzahlen 2012*. Available at:
http://www.cemsuisse.ch/cemsuisse/index.html [accessed 01
January 2013].

Chetty, S., and Campbell, H.C., 2003. *Paths to internationalization among small and medium-sized firms: a global versus regional approach.* European Journal of Marketing, Vol. 37, pp. 796-820.

CIA World Factbook, 2012. *Vietnam.* Available at: https://www.cia.gov/library/publications/the-world-factbook/geos/vm.html [accessed 13 December 2012].

Communicaid Group Ltd., 2009. *Doing Business in Vietnam. Vietnamese Social and Business Culture.* Available at: http://www.communicaid.com/access/pdf/library/culture/doing-business-in/Doing%20Business%20in%20Vietnam.pdf [accessed December 13 2012].

Conner, K., 1991. *A historical comparison of resource-based theory and five schools of thought within industrial organization economics: do we have a new theory of the firm?.* Journal of Management, Vol. 17, No. 1, pp. 121-54.

Coviello, N. and McAuley, A., 1993. *Internationalization and the Smaller Firm: A Review of Contemporary Empirical Research.* Management International Review, Vol. 39, No. 3, pp. 223-256.

Crick, D., 1995. *An investigation into the targeting of U.K. export assistance.* European Journal of Marketing. Vol.29, No.8, pp.79-98.

Crick, D., 1995. *An investigation into the targeting of UK export assistance.* European Journal of Marketing, Vol. 29, No. 8, pp. 76-94.

Czinkota, M., 1982. *Export Development Strategies: U.S. Promotion Policy.* New York: Praeger.

Demick, D. and O'Reilly, A., 2000. *Supporting SME Internationalization: A Collaborative Project for Accelerated Export Development.* Irish Marketing Review Vol.13, No.1, pp.34-35. Available at: http://arrow.dit.ie/cgi/viewcontent.cgi?article=1025&context=jou imriss&sei-redir=1&referer=http%3A%2F%2Fscholar.google.ch%2Fscholar %3Fhl%3Den%26q%3Dsme%2Bexport%26btnG%3D%26as_sd t%3D1%252C5%26as_sdtp%3D#search=%22sme%20export%2 2 [accessed 12 October 2012].

Dhanaraj, C. and Beamish, W., 2003. *A resource-based approach to the study of export performance.* Journal of Small Business Management, Vol.41, No.3, pp.242–261.

Dubini, P. and Aldrich, H., 1991. *Personal and extended networks are central to the entrepreneurial process.* Journal of Business Venturing. Vol.6, pp.13-305.

Dunning J. H., 1993. *Multinational Enterprise in the Global Economy.* Wokingham

Erramilli, M.K. and Rao, C.P., 1990. *Choice of Foreign Market Entry Modes by Service Firms: Role of Market Knowledge.* Management International Review Vol. 30, No. 2, pp.135-150.

ESRC, 2005.*Research Ethics Framework.* Available at: http://www.esrc.ac.uk/ESRCInfoCentre/Images/ESRC_Re_Ethic s_Frame_tcm6-11291.pdf [accessed 5 December 2006].

European Commission, 2005. *The new SME definition – User guide and model declaration.* Enterprise and Industry Publications. Available at: http://www.euresearch.ch/index.php?id=266 [accessed 11 October 2012].

Fernandez-Ortiz, R., & Lombardo, G. F., 2009. *Influence of the capacities of top management on the internationalization of SMEs.* Entrepreneurship & Regional Development: An International Journal, Vol. 21, No. 2, pp. 131–154.

Fillis, I., 2001. *Small firm internationalization: an investigative survey and future research directions*, Management Decision, Vol. 39, No. 9, pp. 767 – 783.

Ford, D., et. al., 2002. *Understanding Business Marketing and Purchasing.* London: Thomson.

Foss, N.J., et. al., 1995. *Resources, Firms and Strategies: A Reader in the Resource-Based Perspective*, Oxford: Oxford University Press, pp. 173-86.

Francis, J. and Collins-Dodd, C., 2004. *Impact of export promotion programs on firm competencies, strategies and performance: The case of Canadian high-technology SMEs.* International Marketing Review, Vol. 21, No. 4/5, pp. 474 – 495.

Gemunden, H., 1991. *Success factors of export marketing: A meta-analytic critique of the empirical studies.* In: Paliwoda, S. et. al., New perspectives on international marketing. pp. 33–62. London: Routledge.

Genctürk, E. and Masaaki, K., 2001. *The Effect of Export Assistance Program Usage on Export Performance: A Contingency Explanation.* Journal of International Marketing Vol. 9, No. 2, pp.51-72. Available at: http://www.jstor.org/discover/10.2307/25048850?uid=42218&uid=3737760&uid=42207&uid=2&uid=3&uid=5911624&uid=67&uid=62&sid=21100994037833 [accessed 21 August 2012].

Genctürk, F. and Kotabe, M., 2001. *The effect of export assistance program usage on export performance: A contingency explanation.* Journal of International Marketing, Vol.9, No.2, pp.51–72.

Gray, J., 1997. *Profiling managers to improve export promotion targeting.* Journal of International Business Studies, Vol.28, No.2, pp.387–420.

Hollesen, S., 2001. *Global Marketing: A Market-responsive Approach.* 2nd ed. Europe: Prentice Hall.

Jansson, H. and Sandberg, S., 2007. *Internationalization of small and medium sized enterprises in the Baltic Sea Region.* Journal of International Management Vol. 14, pp. 65-77.

Jansson, H., 2007. *International business marketing in emerging country markets: the third wave of internationalization of firms.* Cheltenham: Edward Elgar.

Johanson, J. and Wiedersheim-Paul, F., 1975. *The internationalization of the firm, four Swedish case studies.* Journal of Management Studies. Vol. 12, pp.22-305

Johanson, J., and Vahlne, J.-E., 1977. *The internationalization process of the firm: A model of knowledge development and increasing foreign market commitments*. Journal of International Business Studies, Vol. 8, No. 1, pp. 23-32.

Johanson, J., Vahlne, J.E., 2003. *Business relationship learning and commitment in the internationalization process*. Journal of International Entrepreneurship. Vol. 1, pp.83–101.

Kwintessential, 2012. *Vietnam – Language, Culture, Customs and Etiquette*. Available at: http://www.kwintessential.co.uk/resources/global-etiquette/vietnam.html [accessed 13 Dezember 2012].

Lafarge, 2012. *Marktüberblick Zement*. Available at: http://www.lafarge.de/wps/portal/de/1_2_2-Markt_Zement [accessed 02 January 2013].

Lages, F. and Montgomery, B., 2001. *Export assistance, price adaptation to the foreign market, and annual export performance improvement*: A structural model examination. The Economist, Vol.16, pp.88–108.

Leonidou, C., 2004. *An analysis of the barriers hindering small business export development*. Journal of Small Business Management, Vol.42, No.3, pp.279–302.

Lindorff, M., 2007. *The Ethical Impact of Business and Organizational Research: the Forgotten Methodological Issue?*. The Electronic Journal of Business Research Methods Vol. 5, Iss. 1, pp. 21 – 28.

Available at: http://www.ejbrm.com/volume5/issue1/p21 [accessed 12 November 2012].

Loane, S. and Bell, J., 2011. *Awakening dragons: an exploration of the internationalisation of Chinese SMEs from the electronics sector, in Shaoming Zou, Huifen Fu* (ed.) International Marketing (Advances in International Marketing, Volume 21), Emerald Group Publishing Limited, pp.1-31.

Lyles, M., Baird, I., Burdeane, J., Orris, B. and Kuratko D., 1993. *Formalizing planning in small business: increasing strategic choices*. Journal of Small Business Management. April, pp. 38-50.

Mann, M. H., 1966. *Seller Concentration, Barriers to Entry and Rates of Return in Thirty Industries,* 1950-1960. Review of Economics and Statistics, Vol. 48, pp. 296-307.

Mascarenhas, B., 1982. *Coping with Uncertainty in International Business*, Journal of International Business Studies (Fall), pp. 87-98.

McNaughton, R. and Bell, J., 1999. *Brokering networks of small firms to generate social capital for growth and internationalization*. In: Wright, W. et. al. *International Entrepreneurship: Globalization and Emerging Businesses*. Research in Global Strategic Management. Vol.7, pp.63-84. Greenwich: JAI Press.

Miesenbock, K.J., 1988. *Small business and exporting: a literature review*. International Small Business Journal, Vol. 6, No. 2, pp. 42-61.

Mindtools, 2012. *Porter's Five Forces*. Available at:
http://www.mindtools.com/pages/article/newTMC_08.htm
[accessed 02 January 2013].

Ministry of Planning and Investment Vietnam, 2001. *Decree on Support
for Development of Small- and Medium-sized Enterprises*
(Hanoi,), chap. 1, art. 3

Mitchell, O. and Bradley, M., 1986. *Export commitment in the firm –
strategic or opportunistic behavior.* Journal of Irish Business and
Administrative Research. Vol.8, No.2, pp.12-19.

Montgomery, C.A. and Wernerfelt, B., 1988. *Diversification, Ricardian
rents and Tobin's q.* The RAND Journal of Economics, Vol. 19,
No. 4, pp. 623-632. Available at:
http://www.jstor.org/discover/10.2307/2555461?uid=3737760&u
id=2&uid=4&sid=21101001605453 [accessed 25 August 2012].

Naidu, G.M. and Prasad, K., 1994. *Predictors of export strategy and
performance of small and medium firms.* Journal of Business
Research. Vol.31, No.2-3, pp.15-107

Nazar, M. S. and Saleem, H. M., 2009. F*irm-Level Determinants OF
Export Perfomance.* International Business & Economics
Research Journal, Vol. 8, No. 2, pp. 105-112.

Nguyen, T. H., Alam, Q., Perry, M. and Prajogo, D., 2009. *The
Entrepreneurial Role of the State and SME Growth in Vietnam.*
JOAAG, Vol.4, No.1. Available at: http://joaag.com/uploads/6_-
_4_1___NguyenFinal.pdf [accessed 30 December 2012].

Oviatt, B. M., and McDougall, P. P., 1994. *Toward a theory of international new ventures*. Journal of International Business Studies, Vol. 25, No. 1, pp. 45-64.

Peng, W. and Ilinitch, Y., 1998. *Export intermediary firms: A note on export development research*. Journal of International Business Studies, Vol.29, No.3, pp.609–620.

Penrose, E., 1959. *The Theory of the Growth of the Firm*, Oxford: Oxford University Press.

Pointon, T., 1978. *Measuring the gains from government export promotion*. European Journal of Marketing, Vol.12, No.6, pp.451–462.

Porter, M., 1980, *Industry Structure and Competitive Strategy: Keys to Profitability*. Financial Analysis Journal, Vol. 36, pp. 30-41. Competitive Strategy. New York: The Free Press.

Ramaswami, N. and Yang, Y., 1990. *Perceived barriers to exporting and export assistance requirements*. In: Cavusgil, T. and Czinkota, R. et. al. International perspectives on trade promotion and assistance. Westport, CT: Greenwood Press, Inc.

Reid, D., 1984. *Information acquisition and export entry decisions of small firms*. Journal of Business Research. Vol.12, No.2, pp.62-451.

Runckel, C.W., 2011. *Small and Medium Enterprise in Vietnam*. Available at: http://www.business-in-asia.com/vietnam/sme_in_vietnam.html [accessed 30 December 2012].

Rutihinda, C., 2008. *Factors Influencing The Internationalization of Small and Medium Size Enterprises.* International Business & Economics Research Journal Vol.7, No. 12, pp. 45-54.

Ruzzier, M., Antoncic, B. and Konecnik, M., 2006. *The Resource-based Approach to the Internationalization of SMEs: Differences in Resource Bundles between Internationalized and Non-Internationalized Companies.* Zagreb International Review of Economics & Business. Vol. 9, No. 2, pp. 95-116 Available at: http://www.mitjaruzzier.com/konecnik/dokumenti/File/Clanki/Th e_resource_based_approach_to_the_internationalization_of_SM Es.pdf [accessed 05 September 2012]

Ruzzier, M., Hisrich, R.D. and Antoncic, B., 2006. *SME internationalization research: past, present, and future.* Journal of Small Business and Enterprise Development, Vol. 13, No. 4, pp. 476 – 497.

Seerat, F., Mujahid, A. and Sheraz, A., 2011. *Network Classsification on the Basis of Funcitons They Perform and Its Relationship with Internationalization Process of SMEs in Developing Countries – Exploratory Research on Pakistan* [pdf] Australian Journal of Business and Management Research, Vol.1, No.8, pp.35-53. Available at: http://www.ajbmr.com/articlepdf/AJBMR_18_04i1n8a6c.pdf [accessed 16 August 2012].

Seringhaus, R. and Rosson, J., 1991. *Export development and promotion: The role of public organizations.* Boston, MA: Kluwer.

Seringhaus, R., 1986. *The impact of government export marketing assistance*. International Marketing Review Summer, pp.55–66.

Shaw, V. and Darroch, J., 2004. *Barriers to Internationalization: A Study of Entrepreneurial New Ventures in New Zealand*. Journal of International Entrepreneurship. Vol. 2, No.4, pp. 327-343.

Shepherd, W., 1979. *The Economics of Industrial Organization*. Englewood Cliffs, NJ: Prentice-Hall, Inc.

Spence, M., 2003. *Evaluating Export Promotion Programmes: U.K. Overseas Trade Missions and Export Performance*. Small Business Economics Vol. 20, No. 1, pp.83-103.

Su'rez-Ortega, S., 2003. *Export barriers: Insights from small and medium-sized firms*. International Small Business Journal, Vol.21, No.4, pp.403–419.

Terpstra,V.: Sarathy,R.: (2000) *International Marketing*. 8th Edition. Dryden Press

Walters, P., 1983. *Export information sources – A study of their usage and utility*. International Marketing Review. Vol.1, No.2, pp.34-43.

Welch, L. S., and Luostarinen, R., 1988. *Internationalization: evolution of a concept. Journal of General Management*, Vol. 14, No. 2, pp. 34-55.

Wernerfelt, B., 1997. *A resource-based view of the firm*. In: Foss, N.J. (Ed.), Resources, Firms and Strategies: A Reader in the Resource-Based Perspective, Oxford : Oxford University Press, pp. 117-30.

Wilkinson, T. and Brouthers, L., 2000. *An Evaluation of State Sponsored Promotion Programs*. Journal of Business Research. Vol.47, No. 3, pp.229-236. Available at: http://www.sciencedirect.com/science/article/pii/S014829639900 0971 [accessed 21 August 2012]

Wilkinson, T. and Brouthers, L., 2006. *Trade promotion and SME export performance*. International Business Review, Vol.15, pp.233-252.

World Bank, 2012. *Vietnam*. Available at: http://data.worldbank.org/country/vietnam#cp_wdi [accessed 13 December 2012].

Yip, G. S., 1982. Barriers to Entry: *A Corporate Strategy Perspective*. Lexington, MA: D. C. Health and Company.

9. Appendices

Market Entry Barriers Literature Review

Barriers	Source	Implications
Cost advantage of incumbents	Bain 1956; Day 1984; Harrigan 1981; Henderson 1984; Lieberman 1987; Porter 1980b; Scherer 1970, 1980; Schmalensee 1981; Weizsacker 1980; Yip 1982a	One of the most important entry barriers, and usually results from economies of scale and learning curve effects.
Product differentiation of incumbents	Bain 1956, 1962; Bass et al. 1978; Hofer and Schendel 1978; Porter 1980b; Schmalensee 1982	Established firms have brand identification and customer loyalties due to advertising, being first in a market, customer service, or product differences.
Capital requirements	Bain 1956; Eaton and Lipsey 1980; Harrigan 1981; Porter 1980b	Need to invest large financial resources in order to compete or enter a market constitutes barrier to entry, and is higher in capital-intensive industries.
Customer switching costs	McFarlan 1984; Porter 1980b	Switching costs prevent the buyer from changing suppliers, and technological changes often raise or lower these costs.
Access to distribution channels	Porter 1980b, 1985	First or early market entrants use intensive distribution strategies to limit the access to distributors for the potential market entrants.
Government policy	Beatty et al. 1985; Dixit and Kyle 1985; Grabowski and Vernon 1986; Moore 1978; Porter 1980b; Pustay 1985	Government limits the number of firms in a market by requiring licenses, permits, etc.
Advertising	Brozen 1971; Comanor and Wilson 1967; Demsetz 1982; Harrigan 1981; Netter 1983; Reed 1975; Reekie and Bhoyrub 1981; Spence 1980	Heavy advertising by firms already in the market increases the cost of entry for potential entrants and affects brand loyalty as well as the extent of economies of scale by causing cost per dollar revenues to decline.
Number of competitors	Harrigan 1981	Market entry is expected to be more likley during periods of increasing incorporations and less likely after a lag, during periods when high numbers of business failures occur.
Research and development	Harrigan 1981; Schmalensee 1983	This barrier is usually short-lived. Incumbent firms may prevent the entry of new firms by investing effectively in R&D, which increases technological scale economies and forces the ongoing industry context to evolve in a way that would make subsequent attempts to enter even more ineffectual.
Price	Needham 1976; Smiley and Ravid 1983	Price warfare can be a significant deterrent to entry, particularly in industries where firms are more likely to lower their prices to fill underutilized plants.
Technology and technological change	Arrow 1962; Ghadar 1982; Porter 1985; Reinganum 1983	Usually present in high technology industries and can actually raise or lower economies of scale, which is one of the major sources of cost advantages.
Market concentration	King and Thompson 1982	The influence and impact of concentration on entry appear to be minimal.
Seller concentration	Bain 1956, 1968; Crawford 1975; Mann 1966	Entry is unlikely to be as easy in highly concentrated as in less concentrated

Market Entry Barriers Literature Review

Barriers	Source	Implications
		markets. The higher the degree of concentration, the greater the effect of barriers on profit; the lower the degree of concentration, the lower the effect of barriers on profit.
Divisionalization	Schwartz and Thompson 1986	Only expected in exceptionally profitable oligopolistic industries. Incumbent firms create new independent divisions more cheaply than potential entrants who must incur additional overhead costs for entry.
Brand name or trademark	Krouse 1984	New entrants to an industry are denied the benefits of brand name created by others as a result of the exclusive rights to use given with a trademark. Usually a weak barrier.
Sunk costs	Baumol and Willig 1981	Contribute to entry barriers that can also give rise to monopoly profit, resource misallocation, and inefficiencies.
Selling expenses	Williamson 1963	Shifts in demand functions can result from selling efforts making market entry endogenous
Incumbent's expected reaction to market entry	Needham 1976; Yip 1982b	May deter market entry only if the incumbent firms are able to influence potential entrants' expectation about the post-entry reaction of the incumbents.
Possession of strategic raw materials	Scherer 1970	Access to strategic raw materials contributes to firms' absolute cost advantages.

Appendix 1. Literature Review of Market Entry Barriers (Source: Karakaya und Stahl, 1989)

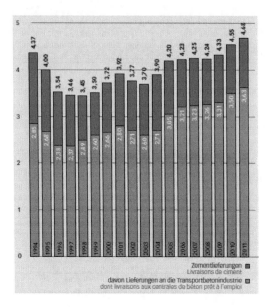

Appendix 2. Delivery of Cement in Switzerland 1994-2011 (Source: CemSuisse, 2012)

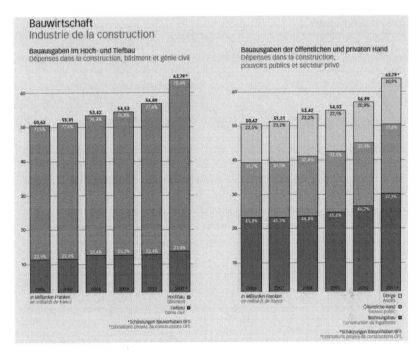

**Appendix 3. Building Industry in Switzerland - Spending 2006-2011
(Sources: CemSuisse, 2012; BFS, 2012)**

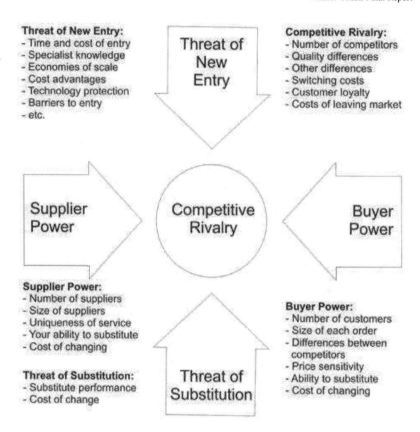

Appendix 4. Porter's Five Forces Model (Source: Mindtools, 2012)

Hypothesis 1	**The support of SME internationalization through networks increases the success of internationalization attempts and confidence of Vietnamese SMEs.**
Hypothesis 2	The need to overcome internal barriers prior to internationalization is highly important and rather underestimated.

Hypothesis 3	SMEs do not follow traditional models of internationalization and therefore are in need of novel supportive approaches.
Hypothesis 4	Important internal barriers are the absence of strategic thinking and planning, limited scale of operations and restricted access to experts and skilled personnel.
Hypothesis 5	Vietnamese SMEs need extensive consultative assistance in preparation for internationalizing to a Western market.
Hypothesis 6	The process of SME internationalization is accompanied by a trade-off between avoiding risk and maintaining high control over the own operations.
Hypothesis 7	The differences in culture, especially business culture, between Vietnamese and Swiss or other European nations pose a significant barrier to internationalization.
Hypothesis 8	The choices and decisions of SMEs during internationalization are highly influenced by the relationship of resource commitment, control over the own operations and perception of risk.

Appendix 5. List of Hypothesis

Steps		Time
Introduce yourself.	o Stanislav Rudnitskiy (interviewer).	
Introduce the project.	**Context of the project:** o Student at FHWN => Master Thesis Research on novel SME Export Concept (Reverse Umbrella Company Concept) o Concept already is proven and exists in supporting Swiss SMEs in foreign markets => Goal is to reverse it and use its advantages to facilitate / support market entry to Switzerland **Goal and main research questions.** o Find out how the existing KTI concept has to be modified to provide reverse support o Test this adaption approach in a case study with Vietnamese Trung Kien Company **Rationale for your study / relevance.** o for individuals – to provide valuable information for further, more in-depth research and analysis in this field. o for organizations – to provide a novel expansion and growth support strategy for SMEs in developing countries; to provide the economy in developed countries with new players, suppliers and healthy competition **What will happen with the results.** o Used to adapt concept, provide starting point for further in depth and quantitative research	
Clarify confidentiality matters and tape recording.	**Clarify confidentiality issues and come to an agreement.** o Myself and the supervisor, Prof. Rolf-Dieter Reineke will have access to the information collected in first place. We will analyze the data for the above-mentioned purposes. o If wished, all names (individuals / companies) will be strictly kept anonymous. **Ask for permission to tape record the interview.** o The reason for doing so is that I would like to transcribe the interviews and analyze them with software for qualitative data analysis. o If there are issues during the conversation of which you think they should be kept off the record,	

	please let us know.
Start with introductory questions.	**Opening questions:** ○ Could you briefly describe your personal background and your current professional role / occupation? ○ Could you briefly describe your involvement and /or interest in this project (concept of promoting export / import)? ○ For how long have you worked with export / import promotion? What is your personal view on: ○ SME Internationalization? ○ Export / import promotion?

Ask your core questions (ca. 6).	**Core Questions**
	1. Peculiarities of Asian **SMEs** as compared to Swiss / Western?
	   a. Innovativeness / know-how
	   b. Readiness for export
	   c. Company structure
	   d. Etc.
	
	2. Peculiarities of Asian **markets** as compared to Swiss / Western markets?
	   a. Competitiveness
	   b. Growth
	   c. Saturation
	   d. Demand
	   e. Etc.
	
	3. What **conclusions** can be drawn from that insight for internationalization?
	
	4. How do SMEs internationalize **nowadays**?
	   a. What **strategy** do they pursue?
	   b. Do they follow **traditional models** of internationalization?
	   c. How is the process?
	   d. What are the incentives?

Page | 2

5. What are basic **requirements** to be able to **internationalize** in the first step and enter **Swiss market** in the second?
a. Structure
b. Product
c. HR
d. Financial => resources
e. Cognitive/Motives
f. Etc.
6. What are barriers for the internationalization of Asian SMEs?
a. What barriers does the **Swiss market** pose for import promotion of Asian SMEs?
b. Internal barriers
7. How can/should an Asian SMEs be supported?
a. What special **demand/requirements** do SMEs have as compared to MNEs?
b. Minimum
c. Optimum
8. Import promotion
a. How do you promote import?
b. Which methods/models/theories do you apply?
c. How could the process be **improved**?
9. What have you heard or can imagine of the traditional **Umbrella Company Concept**?
a. How does this form of internationalization fit in today's **practical internationalization approaches**?
b. **Advantages and disadvantages** compared to traditional methods of internationalization, such as Export, JV, Subsidiary
10. How could you imagine would an export promotion concept using a virtual shared umbrella company work?
a. What could be possible **strengths** of such a concept?
b. What would be possible **weaknesses**?
c. Could you **apply it** in your work?
d. NO => why? What ought to be adapted?
e. YES=> what are the next steps for going over to the next stage?
11. Perspective, development (future outlook)

	12. Future research
Ask how the interview was for the interviewee.	○ Comfort: How was the interview for you? Is there anything you would like to mention additionally?
Clarify further steps.	○ The interviews will be transcribed and analyzed for the purpose of our research.
Say thanks.	What kind of results you expect.

Appendix 6. Interview Guide Version 2

Interviewee: Reverse Umbrella Company Concep

Steps		Time
Make sure your tape works.		
Introduce yourself.	○ Stanislav Rudnitskiy (interviewer).	
Introduce the project.	**Context of the project:** ○ Student at FHWN => Master Thesis Research on novel SME Export Concept (Reverse Umbrella Company Concept) ○ Concept already is proven and exists in supporting Swiss SMEs in foreign markets => Goal is to reverse it and use its advantages to facilitate / support market entry to Switzerland **Goal and main research questions.** ○ Find out how the existing KTI concept has to be modified to provide reverse support ○ Test this adaption approach in a case study with Vietnamese Trung Kien Company **Rationale for your study / relevance.** ○ for **individuals** – to provide valuable information for further, more in-depth research and analysis in this field. ○ for **organizations** – to provide a novel expansion and growth support strategy for SMEs in developing countries; to provide the economy in developed countries with new players, suppliers and healthy competition **What will happen with the results.** ○ Used to adapt concept, provide starting point for further in depth and quantitative research	
Clarify confidentiality matters and tape recording.	**Clarify confidentiality issues and come to an agreement.** ○ Myself and the supervisor, Prof. Rolf-Dieter Reineke will have access to the information collected in first place. We will analyze the data for the above-mentioned purposes. ○ If wished, all names (individuals / companies) will be strictly kept anonymous. **Ask for permission to tape record the interview.**	

	○ The reason for doing so is that I would like to transcribe the interviews and analyze them with software for qualitative data analysis.
	○ If there are issues during the conversation of which you think they should be kept off the record, please let us know.
Start with introductory questions.	**Opening questions:**
	○ Could you briefly describe your personal background and your current professional role / occupation?
	○ Could you briefly describe your involvement and /or interest in this project (concept of promoting export / import)?
	○ For how long have you worked with export / import promotion?
	What is your personal view on:
	○ SME Internationalization?
	○ Export / import promotion?
Ask your core questions (ca. 6).	**Core Questions**
	1. Peculiarities of Asian SMEs as compared to Swiss / Western?
	a. Innovativeness / know-how
	b. Readiness for export
	c. Company structure
	d. Etc.
	2. Peculiarities of Asian markets as compared to Swiss / Western markets?
	a. Competitiveness
	b. Growth
	c. Saturation
	d. Demand
	e. Etc.
	3. What conclusions can be drawn from that insight?
	4. What are basic requirements to be able to internationalize in the first step and enter Swiss market in the second?
	a. Structure

	b. Product
	c. HR
	d. Financial
	e. Cognitive/Motives
	f. Etc.
	5. How can/should an Asian SMEs be supported?
	a. Minimum
	b. Optimum
	6. What have you heard or can imagine of the traditional Umbrella Company Concept?
	7. How does this form of internationalization fit in today's practical internationalization approaches?
	8. What adaptations to the UCC would be necessary to reverse its principle and make it applicable for Asian SMEs wishing to internationalize / export?
	a. What is different as compared to the UCC
	b. What areas have to be adapted =>how
	9. Advantages and disadvantages from perspective of company and from perspective of market
	10. Advantages and disadvantages compared to traditional methods of internationalization, such as Export, JV, Subsidiary...
	11. Perspective, development (future outlook)
	12. Future research
Ask how the interview was for the interviewee.	○ Comfort: How was the interview for you? Is there anything you would like to mention additionally?
Clarify further steps.	○ The interviews will be transcribed and analyzed for the purpose of our research.
Say thanks.	What kind of results you expect.

Appendix 7 Interview Guide Version 1

Stanislav Rudnitskiy	6/7/2013	Page 107 of

Appendix 8 Notes Interview 1

Interview Guide
Reverse Umbrella Company Concept

Context and explanation of the research

This Master Thesis is conducted within the framework of a KTI project with the goal to research an innovative market entry and export method through the establishment of umbrella companies. The project includes the conceptualization and testing of a new innovative concept for lowcost market entry and rapid internationalization of at least 20 Swiss SMEs and start-up companies in the OSEC selected priority countries Indonesia, Kazakhstan, Thailand and Vietnam. The Institute of Management conducts applied research in the conceptual foundation and adaptation to local conditions. OSEC supports the selection of the SMEs and the execution of the empirical studies. The concept is based on the founding of Umbrella Companies invented by United Machinery with partners in target countries. This innovation decreases market entry costs by 40-70% compared to conventional concepts. It also speeds up the realisation of export by 8-12 months with reduced risks. In the last phase of the project, the transferability of the results is tested for other countries and conclusions for strategies and instruments of export promotion will be developed." (FHNW, 2012).

The idea of this Master Thesis Research Project is to reverse the described principle finding a way to modify the Umbrella concept promoting the internationalization of Vietnamese companies to Switzerland and test this approach with the market entry of Trung Kien, a Vietnamese SME, to Switzerland.

Rationale of the study

a. for **individuals** – to provide valuable information for further, more in-depth research and analysis in this field

b. for **organizations** – to provide a novel expansion and growth export strategy for SMEs in developing countries; to provide the economy in developed countries with new players, suppliers and healthy competition

Interview Guide
Reverse Umbrella Company Concept

Interview

1) Could you briefly describe your personal background and your current professional role / occupation?

Attached please find my CV in brief

2) Could you briefly describe your involvement and /or interest in this project (in context of promoting export / import)?

It is really a good project with a number of benefits for non foreign companies to enter into Vietnam market. As a leader of the company, I can support fully for the project both sides, i.e. the fronts and reverse concepts.

3) For how long have you worked with export / import promotion? **3 years**

4) What is your personal view on:

a. SME internationalization? **Good approach to expand markets to gain bigger shares**

b. Export / import promotion? **Promotion will takes time to give overall pictures of your products to export or import, especially offer to the right place for the right products.**

5) What are the peculiarities (e.g. differences) of Asian **markets** as compared to Swiss / Western markets?

a. In terms of competitiveness? **Better prices.**

b. In terms of growth? **Quite high**

c. In terms of saturation? **Average**

d. In terms of demand? **Average**

e. other?

6) What are peculiarities (e.g. differences) of Asian **SMEs** as compared to Swiss / Western SMEs?

a. How does innovativeness / know-how creation differ inside a SME? (Status quo and in e.g. 10 years)? **It is much better in the past, we use more technology and know – how to make products**

b. How ready are Asian SMEs for engaging in export to highly saturated economies, such as Switzerland? **They can offer very competitive price but I am quite worried about the standards.**

Interview Guide
Reverse Umbrella Company Concept

c. What are the major differences in company structure and culture? **Structures are the same, and culture of the family business exist.**

d. What other significant differences can you think of? **Short cut of process and procedures.**

7) What conclusions can be drawn from that insight for the idea of /export promotion? **It is not easy for SMEs to export in term of quality and standards, and capital in this economic crisis.**

8) What are basic requirements to be able to internationalize in the first step and enter Swiss market in the second?

a. Company structure? **BOD, Export Dept, Marketing Dept, Accounting Dept, Admin Dep, Warehouse.**

b. Product? **At least national standards and reach international standards**

c. HR? **Foreign language and knowledge of trade of the client' countries.**

d. Financial? **At least 30 % of revenue per project and the rest can borrowed from the bank.**

e. Cognitive/Motives? **High**

f. Cultural? **Basic**

g. Other?

9) What have you heard of or can imagine of the traditional Umbrella Company Concept? **Yes.**

a. How does this form of internationalization fit in today's practice internationalization approaches? **In theory, it is really good but in practice it is not so easy to start with since marketing and research activities of client countries need to be done before partners are ready to move forward.**

10) What adaptations to the Umbrella Company Concept would be necessary to reverse its principle and made it applicable for Asian SMEs wishing to internationalize / export?

a. What is different as compared to the UCC? **Without clear outcome, Asian SMEs may be afraid of spending initial investments.**

b. What areas have to be adapted anyhow? **Can do the same with UCC.**

Interview Guide
Reverse Umbrella Company Concept

11) What are advantages and disadvantages from perspective of the company (e.g. Trung Kien) and from perspective of market (e.g. Swiss)?

Trung Kien's products are good in term of advantage but capacity to export is low in term of disadvantage and they need to make investments more to increase capacity. The market of Switzerland may also request high standards which the local companies are not easy to fit.

12) What are advantages and disadvantages of the Reverse Umbrella Company Concept compared to traditional methods of internationalization, such as Export, Joint Venture, Wholly owned foreign subsidiary, etc.? **The advantages of RUCC is a test before getting marriage and also reduce risks but the disadvantage of RUCC clients are almost dependant on the representative which may be not capable enough.**

13) How can/should an Asian SMEs be supported during the process of using this concept to start exporting to Switzerland?

a. What are the minimum requirements for successful support? **Standardize production process and knowledge about requirements of products that meet the Swiss standards**

b. What kind of support would be optimal? **Provide demands and price range of products that Switzerland needs.**

14) How do you think will this principle develop, and what is your future outlook for the promotion of export internationally?

a. Please answer this question from a realistic perspective? **We need to do a lot of marketing activities for those who have good products or services to export and it is a good outlook since many Asian SMEs find the ways to develop.**

And

b. From the perspective of the company you would appreciate/wish it to evolve? **If we successfully use UCC first, RUCC is much easier to start with later or at least it can have some financial source to support the marketing and PR for these concepts.**

15) What do you think would be necessary and poignant areas of researching this issue and idea in the future? **We need to find both demands of the two countries and strengths of products and their find markets for them by doing several market researches. How can the development of that concept be supported? The same item b of Q14**

Appendix 9 Mail Interview 2 Vinh (bold=answers)

Appendix 10 Notes Interview 3 Anonymous

Druck: Canon Deutschland Business Services GmbH
Ferdinand - Jühlke - Str. 7· 99095 Erfurt